Fraud Smart

FRAUD SMART

K.H. Spencer Pickett

WILEY

A John Wiley & Sons, Ltd., Publication

Library of Congress Cataloging-in-Publication Data
Pickett, K. H. Spencer.
    Fraud smart / K.H. Spencer Pickett.
        p. cm.
        ISBN 978-0-470-68258-6
    1. Employee theft.   2. Employee crimes–Prevention.   3. Fraud–Prevention.   4. Auditing,
Internal.   I. Title.
    HF5549.5.E43P53 2012
    658.4'73–dc23

                                                             2011044327

ISBN 978-0-470-68258-6 (hbk), ISBN 978-1-119-94477-5 (ebk),
ISBN 978-1-119-96047-8 (ebk), ISBN 978-1-119-96046-1 (ebk)

A catalogue record for this book is available from the British Library.

Typeset in 11/13 pt Times by Toppan Best-set Premedia Limited
Printed in Great Britain by TJ International Ltd, Padstow, Cornwall, UK

Contents

Preface

WHY FRAUD SMART?

After spending a decade performing and managing fraud investigations in a large organization, I spent a further decade delivering regular fraud awareness seminars for groups of non-specialists from many different organizations. My conclusion is that, in most larger organizations, the workforce can be roughly divided into three main groups:

- A small group of individuals who would commit fraud against their employer if given the chance.
- A somewhat larger group of auditors, financial controllers, senior managers and fraud specialists who are actively involved in the fight against fraud.
- And then there is everyone else, who pretty much have little or no interest in the issues raised by workplace fraud as they feel that it has no real relevance to their job.

The first group will gain no benefit from reading this book, as it will not help them plan new frauds. The second group will already have a good knowledge of fraud-related issues and will be aware of the concepts and advice described here. It is the third group who will gain most from reading the book, as a way of getting to grips with fraud by appreciating its potential impact on most organizations.

The aim of the book is simple:

> To move parts of the workforce that are firmly stuck in the third group to becoming Fraud Smart, so that everyone gets involved in the fight against fraud.

From my experience, it is only by involving everyone that we can generate a Fraud Smart workforce who understand the need to take risks, trust their colleagues and drive business success, but are also on guard for dishonesty, whenever and wherever it occurs.

WHAT DOES THE BOOK COVER?

The book is based around a five-part Fraud Smart cycle, which starts with appreciating the risk of fraud and ends with mastering controls over this risk, as set out in Figure 1.

The five-stage Fraud Smart cycle encapsulates our 20 chapters, as is clear from the list of contents. A brief synopsis follows here.

Part I: Understanding the Threat

Chapters 1 to 4 deal with the basic concept of workplace fraud and that the threat of fraud is wide ranging and is a serious concern for almost

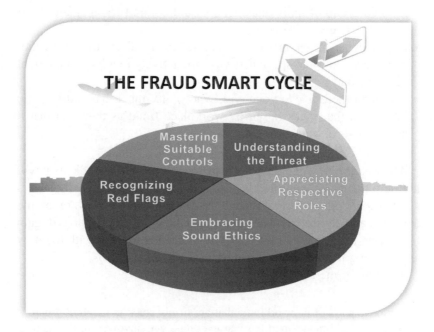

Figure 1 The Fraud Smart cycle.

all organizations, whatever their business and regardless of whether they are private sector, public sector or not-for-profit entities.

Part II: Appreciating Respective Roles

Chapters 5 to 8 consider the roles of different groups within an organization and how they fit together to ensure that fraud is kept on the run. In turn, these expectations can mean that we ask ourselves and our colleagues whether we have the right skill set to cope.

Part III: Embracing Sound Ethics

Chapters 9 to 12 deal with the fundamental concept of business ethics. If we were all honest all of the time, there would be little or no fraud to worry about.

Part IV: Recognizing Red Flags

Chapters 13 to 16 take us into the new role of being proactive about fraud. This calls for Fraud Smart employees who know what to look for and how to report suspicious behaviour.

Part V: Mastering Suitable Controls

Chapters 17 to 20 complete the Fraud Smart cycle by asking that we all get involved in making sure that safeguards against fraud are in place and working. In other words, the risk of fraud should be properly managed alongside the wider business risks that face all organizations.

OUR APPROACH TO PREPARING THE BOOK

To explain our approach, we need to go through some of the principles that we have adopted to help non-specialists become Fraud Smart.

Simple

The book is aimed at managers, supervisors, team leaders and front-line employees who have no specialist knowledge about fraud and fraud control. Each chapter is short and simple and we avoid the use of technical or legal jargon. For example, there is no detailed coverage of fraud investigations as, because of the rigours of the criminal justice system, we do not expect non-specialists to get involved in forensic work. What we do expect is for everyone to appreciate the damage fraud can do, how it occurs, what to look out for and how it may be controlled. Each chapter has a consistent structure that should become familiar as you work through the text.

References

We do not try to document the wise words of the many thousands of experts and knowledgeable specialists in terms of providing a huge list of references throughout the book. This can become offputting; in addition, it is possible to search the websites of the Association of Fraud Examiners, the Institute of Internal Auditors, the larger accounting firms as well as the various accountancy bodies around the world, law enforcement agencies and the many fraud advisory bodies, which will together provide a rich source of information on anti-fraud measures. To keep things manageable, we have drawn from two authoritative sources for our main references, in the section in each chapter entitled 'What Do the Experts Say?'. *Managing the Business Risk of Fraud: A Practical Guide*, sponsored in 2008 by the Institute of Internal Auditors, the American Institute of Certified Public Accountants and the Association of Certified Fraud Examiners, also has an appendix providing a list of useful references for exploring this topic in more detail. *Report to the Nations (On Occupational Fraud and Abuse) 2010 Global Fraud Study* was published by the Association of Certified Fraud Examiners (ACFE), whose website is dedicated to fighting fraud. Both references can be found at www.acfe.com.

Illustrations

There are thousands of frauds reported in the press, in specialist books and in articles on the subject. We have chosen not to fill the book with endless examples using detailed case studies that can become tedious. Our approach has been to note a few illustrative (rather than factual) cases from the UK and the USA, in the section 'What Can Go Wrong?'. Again, having had your appetite stimulated, you can go on to explore documented past cases using any basic search engine.

Toolkits

Each part of the book's Fraud Smart cycle has a closing chapter on 'Building Your Fraud Smart Toolkit'. This uses the conclusions from each chapter to work out what you can do to respond to the issues that have been raised, as part of your personal development strategy.

Models

Most chapters contain a simple model that is used as a frame to address the main issues that are being considered. This is a useful tool for creating some structure to the discussion and the models are designed to aid understanding rather than contain complex detail, in line with our promise to keep things simple.

Consistency

Each chapter has a similar structure to help instil a feeling of familiarity.

Self-Assessment

We have designed a set of multichoice questions that will help you assess the extent to which you have benefited from reading the book. The answers can be found in Appendix B. Please have a go at these questions and record your score in Appendix C.

You can use this book as a basic introduction to the topic, and as a springboard to inspire you to attend training, read more detailed books and delve further into the threat from fraud at work and how this threat can be better managed. We hope that you can work through this book and reflect on ways in which you can sharpen your level of personal alertness and become Fraud Smart.

PART I
Understanding the Threat

Learning Objective

To give you a good appreciation of the threat of fraud and its potential impact on an organization.

1
What Do We Mean by Fraud?

Fraud can involve mundane activities such as employees regularly taking home small items of office equipment, right through to complex schemes established by executive directors for manipulating the financial statements to pump up the share price of their failing company. In this book we are mainly concerned with employee fraud, which affects small businesses, larger companies, public-sector organizations and the many types of not-for-profit entities that exist in developed and developing countries across the world. Our goal is to help raise awareness among non-specialists to help get everyone involved in the fight against fraud. Organizations that succeed in fighting fraud will benefit, while those that do not may well see their reputations suffer as they become targets of their own employees and even of outsiders, who launch attacks either alone or by colluding with these employees.

One argument suggests that fraud against businesses and government agencies is growing at an alarming rate and we now need to take a firm stance or suffer the consequences. This book is based around the Fraud Smart cycle, which covers five key aspects of helping non-specialists get to grips with fraud at work, as set out in Figure 1.1.

This chapter sits within the first part of the Fraud Smart cycle, Understanding the Threat, and provides an outline of some of the more common types of fraud.

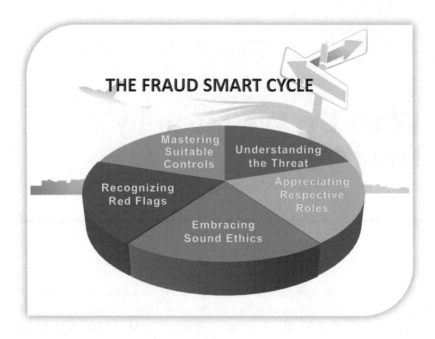

Figure 1.1   The Fraud Smart cycle.

WHAT CAN GO WRONG?

If we fail to get a handle on fraud, there is much that could go wrong. In the past, on discovering that one of their employees was acting in a dishonest manner many organizations would seek out the easiest way to get rid of the problem. This often involved a secretive meeting with the employee, the manager and someone from human resources to force the culprit's resignation, so that he or she would simply go away, as would the problem. A successful outcome would mean that some kind of repayment might be secured and the whole affair would be hushed up. This 'old-style' solution meant that there was no need to ensure that employees were aware of the potential for fraud, or indeed to design any fraud-management process. Bad apples would be quietly removed and it was business as usual, with any losses simply written off, while the culprit would often seek out a new victim.

We can consider the way in which problems can arise by looking at two brief illustrative case studies taken from the UK and the USA. To set the scene, we can turn to the *Times* newspaper for inspiration:

> Frauds, like economies go in cycles. As boom turns to bust, frauds emerge with the inevitability of a hangover after a party. During the

celebrations, there are more opportunities to pick pockets and less chance of getting caught. In the cold light of day, people check their wallets and call the police. With the economic boom coming to a crashing end, the wave of frauds has arrived right on cue.

David Wighton, Business and City Editor,
The Times, December 20 2008, News, page 3

High-powered people can get together and plan to defraud a funding body:

CASE STUDY

Three company directors of a training company were given prison sentences for rigging trainee course attendance numbers to gain Learning Skills Council funds. Two people operating a training consultancy as shadow directors admitted a conspiracy to defraud another organization which made funds available to firms in the region, on behalf of the Learning Skills Council. Another registered director admitted a failure to keep accurate accounting records in breach of companies legislation.

A manager who has a responsible position can abuse this position and, along with others, commit fraud:

CASE STUDY

A hospital manager and four other people were sentenced for conspiring to defraud a hospital trust of £580 000. The manager pleaded guilty to conspiracy to defraud and was jailed for three years. Two other defendants were sentenced for conspiracy to defraud, and a further two for money laundering offences. All were given prison sentences. The fraud was uncovered by finance staff and the police discovered that over half a million pounds had been defrauded from the payroll system. The manager was found to have used her position of responsibility to create 'ghost' employees who she pretended had worked shifts as administrative and clerical staff. After the wages for these false shifts had been paid to the other defendants, the manager attempted to cover this up by deleting the phantom shifts from the payroll list. Her actions left an electronic 'footprint' in the system which could be traced back to her.

The 'sweep it under the carpet' approach no longer works, as this simply encourages dishonesty if the only sanction when caught is enforced resignation. The threat of fraud has grown not only due to the economic downturn but also because management layers have been removed, and low-paid junior staff now have much more responsibility, including instant access to customer information as online commerce becomes the norm. We can mix into this potent cocktail the fact that people frequently move jobs and often have no time to bond with their employer and create strong ties of loyalty. Meanwhile, organized crime gangs have replaced their guns with virtual but much more lethal weapons in the form of online access to try to defraud large organizations.

There is no way to combat these developments other than by making sure that the workforce throws itself into fraud control and by installing a robust anti-fraud strategy. Any failure to do so may result in a vulnerable business being subject to continual fraud and abuse, and staff as well as customers becoming demoralized by a poor corporate reputation. It does not stop there, however, as a further trend is for companies to be fined if they fail to control fraud in an appropriate manner.

WHAT DO THE EXPERTS SAY?

As explained in the Preface, we have drawn from two main sources of expertise to help explain Fraud Smart management, as follows:

- *Managing the Business Risk of Fraud: A Practical Guide*, sponsored in 2008 by the Institute of Internal Auditors, The American Institute of Certified Public Accountants and the Association of Certified Fraud Examiners. We will refer to this guide as the 'MBRF'.
- *Report to the Nations (On Occupational Fraud and Abuse) 2010 Global Fraud Study*, published by the Association of Certified Fraud Examiners. We will refer to this extensive survey of fraud across the world as the 'ACFE Report'.

These two publications contain extremely useful guidance and some of the extracts that are relevant to this chapter are noted. We start with a definition of fraud taken from *Managing the Business Risk of Fraud: A Practical Guide*:

Fraud is any intentional act or omission designed to deceive others, resulting in the victim suffering a loss and/or the perpetrator achieving a gain. (MBRF, page 5)

The guide goes on to warn about the menace from uncontrolled fraud:

All organizations are subject to fraud risks. Large frauds have led to the downfall of entire organizations, massive investment losses, significant legal costs, incarceration of key individuals, and erosion of confidence in capital markets. Publicized fraudulent behavior by key executives has negatively impacted the reputations, brands, and images of many organizations around the globe. (MBRF, page 5)

We can turn now to the *Report to the Nations* for a frightening estimate of the scope of fraud internationally:

Survey participants estimated that the typical organization loses 5% of its annual revenue to fraud. Applied to the estimated 2009 Gross World Product, this figure translates to a potential total fraud loss of more than $2.9 trillion. (ACFE Report, page 4)

This sky-high figure of a $2.9 trillion potential loss sets the scene for the rest of the book. We return to this report for more information on the quoted figure:

Asset misappropriation schemes were the most common form of fraud in our study by a wide margin, representing 90% of cases – though they were also the least costly, causing a median loss of $135,000. Financial statement fraud schemes were on the opposite end of the spectrum in both regards: These cases made up less than 5% of the frauds in our study, but caused a median loss of more than $4 million – by far the most costly category. Corruption schemes fell in the middle, comprising just under one-third of cases and causing a median loss of $250,000. (ACFE Report, page 4)

You can see from these statistics that fraud is not harmless, victimless and therefore of low concern. It is unfair, since it diverts funds from the people and entities that have a legal right to those funds. Moreover, it has been found that fraud can be used by organized crime to fund other serious offences such as drug dealing and people trafficking. In some cases an entire business can collapse if it has been defrauded by an employee. There is good reason for employees, partners, associates and customers at all levels to help combat fraud as far as possible.

OUR MODEL EXPLAINED

We have developed a simple model, shown in Figure 1.2, to illustrate one way of dealing with the issues raised in this chapter.

Our model suggests that we can view fraud as affecting at least four main aspects of an organization: its income received, its spending, its data (or information) and its assets. We can explore these issues by briefly considering each separate part of our model in turn.

Income

Income is an obvious target for fraudsters, in the sense that if it can be diverted into someone else's bank account then it becomes the income

Figure 1.2   Types of fraud.

of the beneficiary. In one case cheques due to the company were intercepted by postroom staff and given to a criminal gang, whose members altered the payee and paid them into a specially established bank account. An even better fraud involved the gang setting up bank accounts in the same name as the company so that stolen cheques could be banked unaltered.

Income is thus due to the company but diverted to the fraudster. One problem for the fraudster can occur when the company continues to chase the debtor and the fraud eventually comes to light.

There are several questions that can be asked to assess how far income could be at risk, including:

• Do we have processes that involve receiving cash in such a way that it could be misappropriated?
• Is there a source of income for which records could be falsified?
• Is there a source of income such as donations or refunds that are not expected by the company and that could be diverted?
• Could an employee arrange to write off debt so that if it is later received, it can be fraudulently diverted without any obvious gaps in the account?

All income belongs to the organization and it is at risk if it is not carefully controlled. The issue is whether the controls are sound enough to protect all sources of revenue. The key question to ask is: Can funds due to the organization be intercepted and diverted?

Expenditure

Expenditure is also a target, in that fraudsters will try to achieve payment to themselves (or an associate) by diverting funds so that they fall under their control. A clever accounts staffer may be able to invent false supplier accounts as well as their own special bank account and arrange one or more payments from the company. Bid rigging, where contractors conspire to set the rates for projects that a company is letting, means that the company in question will not achieve value for money and will end up spending more on its contracts. One reprographics manager set up a printing company and then sent out subcontracted jobs to this same company. Meanwhile, he did the jobs himself by using his employer's printing facilities at weekends, which he also claimed as overtime.

There are several questions that can be asked to assess how far expenditure could be at risk, including:

* Could someone falsify their qualifications and thereby earn more money than they otherwise should have?
* Could someone falsify their timesheet, overtime claim, expenses or performance figures to earn extra income?
* Could a fabricated order be placed that leads to a fraudulent payment being generated?
* Could duplicate payments be scheduled and one of the duplicates then diverted?

Authorized spending can end up in a fraudster's account if it is diverted there, while unauthorized spending can be generated by circumventing disbursement controls. The key question to ask is: Can payments be activated so that they end up in a fraudster's account or be misapplied in any way?

Assets

The theft of corporate assets can be widespread in companies that hold equipment, inventory and stocks of finished goods. This is an age-old problem. The theft of cash bags is a further problem if the organization has cash receipting and movement systems in place. Misuse of company resources is a different type of problem, where in extreme cases an employee may run their own business using company facilities. One manager of a children's home over-ordered food supplies and his deputy and caretaker would help him take home the excess food once or twice a week. Meanwhile, the manager's wife ran a catering firm and used this food to reduce her outgoings.

There are several questions that can be asked to assess how far assets could be at risk, including:

* Could equipment be removed from office premises without authorization?
* Could stationery be removed on a regular basis?
* Could office resources be used to support a private business?
* Could corporate information systems be breached and the underlying data stolen?

- Could corporate assets be over-stated on the balance sheet to give a misleading impression to users?

Many organizations have an edge over their competition through the information they hold on markets, financial products, partners and customers. Together with other assets, this information can be at risk.

The key question to ask is: What assets are at risk and could they be accessed in an inappropriate manner?

Data

Data, information and company intelligence present a growing problem in terms of the fraud angle. Straight data loss is an issue that is compounded where these data can be used to perpetrate fraud. In fact, there is a black market in personal data that can be used by opportunist fraudsters, who access the files and pass on relevant data relating to personal and financial details to criminal gangs who can take advantage of the facility.

Banking details, national insurance numbers, addresses, credit details and other personal data are being hoovered up by large organizations to power their customer information systems, but nonetheless pose a threat whenever there is a breach of security. It has been known for customer service employees to photograph customer screens on their mobile phones and pass this information on to outsiders, who create false accounts or address changes to divert funds to their control. Victims of identity theft then face an uphill battle to reinstate their identity and they rightly blame the organization for allowing their details to be stolen.

There are several questions that can be asked to assess how far data could be at risk, including:

- Could personal details be accessed to facilitate identity fraud?
- Could customers' financial details be stolen to commit banking or credit card fraud?
- Could sensitive company knowledge be applied to share dealing based on insider trading?
- Could confidential details of new product designs be stolen?
- Have official-looking emails been received that request user ID and password details, possibly appearing to be from the corporate IT security team?

Data and the more common store of information that 'knowledge-based' companies now harvest are at risk as the increasingly most sought-after aspect of organizational resources. The key question to ask is: How can we protect the vast amount of information held on our corporate and local systems?

There are obvious parts of the organization that are at risk of fraud in all but the smallest of organizations. The sad fact of human nature is that if something can go wrong then at some point in the future it probably will go wrong. One view is that frauds do not just happen, they are *allowed* to happen because no one thought to ask key questions about areas that are at risk.

OUR THREE KEY CONCLUSIONS

There are three main conclusions that we can draw from our discussions and suggestions. These conclusions will be used to drive your Fraud Smart toolkit, which you will be designing at the end of this part of the book:

1.1 Fraud is ever present and is growing in most developed and emerging economies, so that it must be seen as representing a major threat to most organizations in most sectors.
1.2 It is no longer possible to sweep fraud under the carpet, hoping that any incidents can be dealt with by simply asking the culprit to resign.
1.3 Organizations own income, expenditure, assets and data and these are all at risk if there are no effective measures in place to ensure that everyone is Fraud Smart and is operating as a full-time custodian of the corporate resource.

In the end, protecting income, expenditure, assets and data is about protecting the organization's reputation. We said in the Preface that everyone who works for or is associated with a larger organization should appreciate what fraud is and its ramifications. What we need to add now is that this stance is not a *nice-to-have* but more of a *must-have* approach, which means that ideally the entire workforce should possess the basic knowledge conveyed by this book.

2
A Wide Range of Threats

Fraud is not like other risks, as it tends to represent a direct threat to an organization rather than a potential opportunity. Having said that, there is a slight argument that some commonplace frauds, say online fraud or overseas bribes, may be seen as opportunities to gain an edge by allowing an astute company to boast about its safeguards in contrast to the competition.

As we say in Chapter 1, this book is based around the Fraud Smart cycle that covers five key aspects of helping non-specialists get to grips with fraud at work. This is repeated in Figure 2.1.

This chapter sits within the first part of the Fraud Smart cycle, Understanding the Threat, and covers some of the better-known frauds that affect most organizations.

WHAT CAN GO WRONG?

The problem with fraud is that it may not be seen as a real threat. There are several reasons for this. The organization may feel that it is something that happens to other entities, not itself, and some frauds, particularly low-level abuse, are pretty much concealed, in that management does not know they are happening. So the true extent of fraud and the damage it can cause may not be properly acknowledged by senior managers and work teams, who just want to get ahead and not have to worry about too many cumbersome controls. However, if the threat of fraud is not fully appreciated, particularly the more unusual kinds, there is a great deal that could go wrong.

Figure 2.1   The Fraud Smart cycle.

We can consider how problems can arise by looking at several brief illustrative case studies taken from the UK and the USA. The first involved a police officer.

CASE STUDY

A crooked police fraud squad officer who masterminded a multimillion-pound mortgage fraud with the help of his brother and a solicitor's clerk was jailed for nearly six years. The specialist fraud investigator built up a buy-to-let empire during the property boom years. He inflated the price of each house he bought and was granted massive loans by mortgage lenders. Fellow police officers searched his home and found a fake driving licence in the name of a baby who died many years ago. He used a solicitor's clerk to send other solicitors' firms false information and to sign off bogus documents. The case centred around a number of allegations of mortgage fraud where buy-to-let mortgages were obtained by making false statements with regard to the purchase terms of the property. Mortgages worth over £4.5 million were received. In his capacity as a police officer he also certified documents that were used to open a savings account. The judge said: 'The defendant was a serving police officer throughout and that has to be seen as an aggravating factor.'

The 'it could never happen to me' stance can be heart-breaking when it does in fact happen. Doing business with a well-known, tried-and-trusted representative, who is consistently successful among a small group of elite people in the same city, could be seen as one way of ensuring that nothing can go wrong. When this simple business model fails, however, it can have catastrophic effects, as shown by our next case study.

CASE STUDY

A fraud that shook the financial world ended in the imprisonment of Bernard Madoff, who was given the maximum sentence of 150 years in June 2009 for defrauding investors of some $65 billion. The judge at the time noted that the breach of trust was massive, while Madoff apologised for the 'legacy of shame' he had brought on his family and the industry. Thousands of investors succumbed to the so-called Ponzi scheme, which involved using the funds from new investors to pay existing investors, by pretending that the money came from impressive gains because of Madoff's special investment strategy.

Madoff established an investment company to sell stock to rich investors, who trusted him because of his highly respected profile in the investment community; at one point he was chairman of the NASDAQ. He concentrated on the affluent New York business community and existing investors told potential members about the great returns, so the scheme grew quickly. The infamous Charles Ponzi had used a similar approach in the 1920s and, like Madoff, promised amazing returns on investments. No one could work out how Madoff achieved such huge returns despite several investigations by regulators. He shrouded his investment strategy with an air of mystery, and no one could unravel his explanations of why he did so well. It was a family-run business, which meant that there was less scope for whistleblowers to expose the flaws. Moreover, it was felt that since all the clients gained a healthy annual return, regardless how the markets were performing, and since Madoff was such a well-liked person, all was well. In fact, many personal clients felt as if they were members of an elite club that allowed them access to great returns. Madoff defrauded the rich and the famous along with international banks and charities; ordinary working people also suffered.

Fraud occurs wherever it can, and this can be anywhere. Our next example involves a trusted manager who used loose procedures to conspire with an outsider.

CASE STUDY

A manager in the education department at one of Scotland's city councils was charged following a police investigation into allegations of a £300 000 fraud, while another person, not employed by the council, was arrested. The charges relate to invoices for a home tutoring service and the employee had been suspended from his post. A local councillor expressed his view on the matter:

> It is of enormous concern, given the experiences the council has had in recent times. It is my understanding that steps have been taken to improve things radically in the aftermath of the shocking audit report two years ago. But I think we will have to look very carefully to see if enough has been done and to see if more can be done to tighten up on procedures.

Huge amounts can be obtained by simply creating false invoices and seeking to get these paid.

CASE STUDY

Four criminals were jailed over a multimillion-pound fraud. The fraud operated over a period of four years via a number of companies grouped under one name. The defendants extracted large amounts of money from three financial institutions by submitting over 1000 false invoices, totalling over £85 million. Once the fraud was uncovered the fraudulent group of companies went into liquidation. They left the institutional investors victim to a combined net loss of over £7.5 million. All defendants pleaded guilty to several counts of fraudulent trading.

Simple documents such as timesheets can be falsified to create a fraud.

CASE STUDY

A local authority chef has been sentenced to 10 months' imprisonment for deception and false accounting. The fraud came to light when one of the catering managers suspected that the chef was claiming for times when he was not on duty. During the investigation it was discovered that he had altered his timesheets by tampering with the carbon copies, so a different version to that signed off by the manager was sent to the agency, resulting in him being paid for more hours than he worked. The chef pleaded guilty.

Some frauds are not particularly obvious and they can involve an abuse of company resources which goes on for some time.

CASE STUDY

A laboratory technician used his employer's mailing system to deliver a large number of items that he had sold on the Internet. The technician not only conducted auctions on the auction website eBay, but also sent items to buyers using the office postal system. A purchaser spotted the franked packaging and contacted the police, who found that he had conducted over 850 transactions on the site, a large part believed to have been while he was at work. Some items sold were items of laboratory equipment believed to have been stolen from the department in which he worked. A substantial amount of items are believed to have been posted via the employer's post room and at the employer's expense. The technician pleaded guilty to six counts of obtaining services by deception.

WHAT DO THE EXPERTS SAY?

We have already mentioned the threat that fraud poses to larger organizations where there are many offices, hundreds of work teams and complex systems in place. Serious fraudsters go for large money flows or lax systems, as noted in one of our key texts:

The industries most commonly victimized in our study were the banking/ financial services, manufacturing and government/public administration sectors. (ACFE Report, page 4)

However, fraud also has an impact on smaller businesses:

Small organizations are disproportionately victimized by occupational fraud. These organizations are typically lacking in anti-fraud controls compared to their larger counterparts, which makes them particularly vulnerable to fraud. (ACFE Report, page 4)

We are most concerned in this book with employee fraud, which is about dishonestly using one's occupation for personal gain. *Managing the Business Risk of Fraud* classifies occupational fraud risks into three general categories – fraudulent statements, misappropriation of assets and corruption – along with various sub-categories:

1 Intentional manipulation of financial statements, which can lead to:
   a Inappropriately reported revenues.
   b Inappropriately reported expenses.
   c Inappropriately reflected balance sheet amounts, including reserves.
   d Inappropriately improved and/or masked disclosures.
   e Concealing misappropriation of assets.
   f Concealing unauthorized receipts and expenditures.
   g Concealing unauthorized acquisition, disposition, and use of assets.
2 Misappropriation of:
   a Tangible assets by:
      i Employees.
      ii Customers.
      iii Vendors.
      iv Former employees and others outside the organization.
   b Intangible assets.
   c Proprietary business opportunities.
3 Corruption including:
   a Bribery and gratuities to:
      i Companies.
      ii Private individuals.
      iii Public officials.
   b Receipt of bribes, kickbacks, and gratuities.
   c Aiding and abetting fraud by other parties (e.g., customers, vendors). (MBRF, page 24)

The MBRF guide goes on to band the various groups that may be involved in misappropriation:

1 Employees.
   • Creation of, and payments to, fictitious vendors.
   • Payment of inflated or fictitious invoices.
   • Invoices for goods not received or services not performed.
   • Theft of inventory or use of business assets for personal gain.
   • False or inflated expense claims.
   • Theft or use of customer lists and proprietary information.
2 Employees in collusion with vendors, customers, or third parties.
   • Payment of inflated or fictitious invoices.
   • Issuance of inflated or fictitious credit notes.
   • Invoices for goods not received or services not performed.
   • Preferred pricing or delivery.
   • Contract bid rigging.
   • Theft or use of customer lists and proprietary information.
3 Vendors.
   • Inflated or fictitious invoices.
   • Short shipments or substitution of lower quality goods.
   • Invoices for goods not received or services not performed.
4 Customers.
   • False claims for damaged or returned goods or short shipments.
     (MBRF, page 26)

It is clear that a lot could go wrong and many different parties could become involved in deceitful behaviour. We need to make one further point here: we cannot assume that everyone is dishonest all the time. Since the essence of business is based around mutual trust, that would mean that no one would do business with anyone. It is simply the case that deceit could undermine a business relationship; we need to be aware that occasionally people succumb to temptation, and that some do so more readily than others.

OUR MODEL EXPLAINED

We have developed a simple model in Figure 2.2 to illustrate one way of dealing with the issues raised in this chapter.

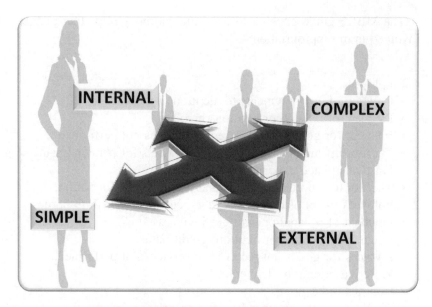

Figure 2.2   Types of threats.

Our model suggests that fraud comes in many forms and guises. It can be simple scams that happen just by chance, or it can be based around intricate webs of deceit that on face value may not appear to be illegal. Fraud can be perpetrated by employees or by criminals with no relationship to the organization. Within the matrix are many different combinations that mean that the threat is ever changing.

The best frauds, from the fraudster's point of view, are those that are not detected and remain hidden for many years. The next best are those that should never have happened, and if revealed would embarrass the managers or even lead to charges of neglect. The threat of fraud can be explored by considering each separate part of our model in turn.

Simple

Some frauds can be so simple that, with hindsight, they should really never have happened:

• One junior accounts clerk's main job was to process a cash-based expenses system for the various teams who covered sales, follow-ups and client visits. Each claim was supported by receipts, some from local restaurants and retail outlets. The accounts clerk simply added in his own receipts and increased the amount payable by a round sum that he forged on the claim form. He then deducted his 'extras' from the cash before paying the balance over to the claimant. The auditors would be presented with the receipts, which would tie up with the cash paid out. This was a simple fraud that was eventually found out.

- Another fraud involved the regular overcharging of overtime claims by a team of drivers who made sure that their claims were consistent – even though they were inflated. This was a simple fraud that also involved false accounting in terms of incorrect claims.
- High-volume, low-level fraud can be dangerous in that the amounts grow over time; if it is left unchecked, it can instil a culture of abuse and scams across the entire workforce. It can also lead to larger frauds where there is a view that 'everyone should have a go'.
- Moreover, people will not blow the whistle on a large fraud when they themselves could be exposed for low-level abuse that they undertake from time to time.

Simple frauds can have a devastating impact. In one cash office, a large amount of cash was collected at the end of a busy shift. Between the time the cash was counted and placed into five cash bags and when these bags were stored and handed over to a mobile security team, one bag disappeared. No amount of CCTV review, interrogation and detailed enquiries over several months could uncover how this bag containing £35 000 disappeared and who took it. Because of lax security and the fact that people were allowed to wander into the cash area throughout the day, the bag was simply swiped when no one was looking.

Complex

On the other side of the model are complex frauds that have been very carefully planned:

- A fraud can arise where key-logging software (or even hardware inserted inside a PC) is used to record the key strokes of operatives, information that is then used to obtain access codes and passwords so that customer accounts can be breached.
- In serious cases, money transfer codes can be recorded and used to transmit funds overseas.

- One canny fraudster pretended to be a government official by paying in £100 to a social services client account. Because the cashier therefore assumed that he was employed by the agency, he was allowed to withdraw £3000 fraudulently from another account without showing proper ID.
- Where executive managers conspire to defraud their company or the investment community, complex arrangements can be employed as a smokescreen to deter any investigation. Where these same managers are able to override established procedures to set up journal transfers of entries in the final accounts, the accounts do not reflect a true and fair view of the business and much can go wrong.

Some complex frauds can be carefully planned. For instance, a fraudster may engage in a series of banking transfers over many months so that this pattern is used to counter controls that are activated for suspect transactions. When a large transfer is then attempted, no flags are raised and the fraudster can divert substantial sums that belong to the victim company.

Internal

We have already said that we are concentrating on employee fraud as a dangerous growth area:

- This is about trusted people, many of whom are in positions of authority, abusing this trust and acting dishonestly. Employees in positions of trust can cause a great deal of damage. They can falsify documents and generate false accounts, which they can then activate. An address field can be altered and expensive goods or a refund cheque delivered to a temporary location that is controlled by the fraudster.
- A dishonest procurement manager can set up overpriced contracts for people he knows and receive a kickback for these favours.
- Organizations that thrive on an open and trusting culture can remove controls and barriers to make it easier for staff to perform and would shy away from accusing employees who are acting suspiciously.
- Many businesses focus on savings and efficiencies when resourcing projects, chasing business and setting up new teams. The problem is that the scope for fraud and corruption may not be on the agenda when establishing resourcing structures.

Where a staff member colludes with an outsider, or for that matter a criminal gang, things could get really complicated, as the insider is able to work around controls to aid the fraud. In fact, some professional criminals plant employees into financial services companies to allow them to understand and get past controls that are meant to protect against these criminal activities.

External

The final part of the model is external fraud; whatever is out there in the world beyond the office space:

- Organized criminals pose a major risk. They target organizations with weaknesses that can be exploited. One simple opportunist fraud involves sending invoices for the supply of small items such as diaries, calendars or local office supplies and hoping that large companies will process the invoices with little or no checking, because the values are so small. A scattergun approach may be used to get, say, 5 per cent of all fraudulent invoices paid by unsuspecting companies or government agencies.
- Blackmail and coercion are well-known tools for extracting money from a company by threatening to publicize confidential information or by damaging corporate resources, including information systems. Many external frauds are aided by an insider, who could actually be a lowly paid worker from the postroom or the buildings security team and provides a way of getting access to company resources.
- Many organizations do not allow customer data to be held on laptops that are taken out of the office and also ban the use of USB data-storage devices. Some companies are asking their staff not to wear their company badge outside work and to watch out for people who seek to socialize with them, say through online social networking, and take an interest in their employer.
- In terms of online social networking, there is an abundance of interaction between people who do not really know each other but who exchange personal information on an ongoing basis. Unfortunately, where dishonesty enters the equation, much could go wrong if precautions are not taken.
- A simple scam was carried out by a small outfit who offered a three-month free trial of its new product, asking the customer to call to cancel the contract at any time before the three months were up. Meanwhile, a direct debit was set up that would activate after the free period. Customers found that they could not contact the company by phone and there was no postal address. Needless to say, the

company started taking the monthly payments after the three months had expired and some banks found it hard to cancel the payments, as there was a legal agreement between the customer and the company.

External fraud can damage a company's reputation. This could happen if a fraudster set up a professonal-looking website that paralleled that of a well-known company and then captured personal data or even accepted payments from unsuspecting customers.

OUR THREE KEY CONCLUSIONS

One view suggests that damaging frauds have either already happened to an organization, will probably happen at some time in the future, or are actually happening but no one (except the culprit) knows. There are three main conclusions that we can draw from our discussions. These conclusions will be used to drive your Fraud Smart toolkit, which you will design at the end of this part of the book:

2.1 There is a wide range of potential deceptions that have to be addressed in the fight against fraud, ranging from financial misstatement and misappropriation through to bribery and corruption.
2.2 The threat of fraud must be understood as ever present if it is to be tackled, and can be simple or complex depending on its nature and the way it is carried out.
2.3 The fact that employees as well as outsiders can commit fraud should be fully recognized, in addition to the most dangerous scenario that occurs where the two groups conspire to act against a business.

It can be seen from this chapter that unfortunately, there are a wide range of people who commit frauds and if they are left unchecked, the types of fraud they are able to commit can be quite imaginative.

3
The Global Scene

We have already said that fraud is ever present as a threat to any organization. This chapter adds the dimension that fraud also has an international dimension that knows no borders. Companies are increasingly doing business with partners, other organizations and customers across the world, often linked through online communications.

As we have seen, the book is based around a Fraud Smart cycle that covers five key aspects of helping non-specialists get to grips with fraud at work. This is repeated in Figure 3.1.

This chapter sits within the first part of the Fraud Smart cycle, Understanding the Threat, and covers the international dimension of some fraud, which makes it even harder to identify the source.

WHAT CAN GO WRONG?

Global fraud creates many problems, especially since the company, its stakeholders, the customers, fraudsters and law enforcement agencies may be based in different countries with different legal or regulatory regimes. Complex frauds can arise when the perpetrator knows that there is poor communication between the country they reside in and the country in which the victim organization is based. Most jurisdictions are loath to abide by rules created by other jurisdictions and there may well be some friction between countries that are not used to cooperating with each other. If we fail to recognize the global repercussions of some frauds, this could cause significant difficulties.

Figure 3.1 The Fraud Smart cycle.

We can consider the way in which problems are able to arise by looking at several brief illustrative case studies taken from the UK and the USA. The first had a global impact.

CASE STUDY

'Liar loans' had international ramifications and eventually led to the credit crunch. These loans were granted without proof of income and often using false disclosures to secure the funds required for a house purchase. They were negotiated by loans officers on the basis of application forms signed by the various applicants as a true disclosure of their financial circumstances. Many applications were bordering on fraudulent and were in direct conflict with the basic rules of credit assessment and underwriting principles. Most ended in foreclosure when the borrower could not repay the monthly amount due. As the US housing market collapsed and the derivative securities based on bad mortgages spread across the globe, financial markets around the world started to unravel.

Cyber-fraud is a major threat and consists of fraudsters exploiting the anonymity of the Internet and the confusion over cross-border jurisdictions to commit their crimes:

CASE STUDY

Fraudsters hacked into an international bank's database and stole the credit card details and other personal data of thousands of customers. They then sold this information to international criminals who specialized in credit card fraud.

A sad but growing fraud that touches many countries involves the fraudster masquerading as someone else to earn the trust of an unsuspecting victim:

CASE STUDY

A fraudster based in West Africa earned the trust of a lonely grandmother who lived in the UK by pretending to be a good-looking ex-serviceman from the US army. This Internet relationship lasted for some time before the 'ex-serviceman' claimed that he had fallen on hard times and managed to extract £80 000 from his new-found British friend.

It is not just individuals, multinational companies can also commit fraud and this can have repercussions across the business world:

CASE STUDY

Tyco International has operations in over 100 countries and claims to be the world's largest maker and servicer of electrical and electronic components. Since 1986, Tyco has claimed over 40 major acquisitions as well as many minor acquisitions. The corporation's former CEO, CFO and General Counsel were accused of giving themselves

(Continued)

interest-free or very low-interest loans (sometimes disguised as bonuses) that were never approved by the board or repaid. They were also accused of selling their company stock without telling investors, which is a requirement under SEC rules. As many as 40 Tyco executives took loans that were later 'forgiven' as part of the organization's loan-forgiveness programme, although it was said that many did not know they were doing anything wrong. Hush money was also paid to people whom the company feared would 'rat out' the main suspects, who concealed their illegal actions by keeping them out of the accounting books and away from the eyes of shareholders and board members.

WHAT DO THE EXPERTS SAY?

In considering what our two key texts have to say on global deception, we start with the view that fraud is fraud no matter the country or the jurisdiction:

> Occupational fraud is a global problem. Though some of our findings differ slightly from region to region, most of the trends in fraud schemes, perpetrator characteristics and anti-fraud controls are similar regardless of where the fraud occurred. (ACFE Report, page 5)

Anti-corruption legislation is notoriously difficult to interpret when companies are operating in countries where sweeteners are the norm. *Managing the Business Risk of Fraud* provides some timely guidance on this matter:

> Organizations that have operations outside their home countries need to consider other relevant anti-corruption laws when establishing a fraud risk management program. Transparency International, a multinational organization focused on anti-corruption and transparency in business and government, issues an annual Corruption Perception Index, which ranks countries on their perceived levels of corruption. The Corruption Perception Index can assist organizations in prioritizing their anti-corruption efforts in areas of the world at greatest risk. It must be remembered, of course, that corruption can also occur in an organization's home country. (MBRF, page 26)

The other point to note relates to the impact of the Internet on white-collar crime:

Keep in mind, cyber fraudsters do not even have to leave their homes to commit fraud, as they can route communications through local phone companies, long-distance carriers, Internet service providers, and wireless and satellite networks. They may go through computers located in several countries before attacking targeted systems around the globe. What is important is that any information – not just financial – is at risk, and the stakes are very high and rising as technology continues to evolve. (MBRF, page 27)

OUR MODEL EXPLAINED

We have developed a simple model, outlined in Figure 3.2, to illustrate one way of dealing with the issues raised in this chapter.

Our model suggests that all organizations need to think through the way in which their domestic arrangements interface with their global presence in terms of the relationships they might have with overseas territories. These relationships are designed to promote succesful business growth by exploiting foreign markets, but they also introduce

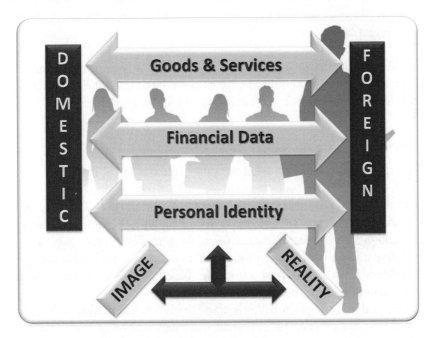

Figure 3.2   Types of fraud.

the scope for foreign fraudsters to exploit these relationships in a deceitful manner. Cyber-terrorism is an adjunct to e-fraud, as governments as well as corporate bodies think through their protection against sabotage and blackmail, which in extreme cases can seek to undermine whole economies.

Staying with the more straightforward corporate fraud angle, we can explore these issues by considering each separate part of our model in turn.

Domestic

Each country that trades internationally needs to have its own domestic arrangements to protect customers wherever they reside:

- It also needs a set of protocols to deal with frauds that cross national borders and even continents.
- It is a fact that many companies have bases in different countries around the world. There needs to be coordination to ensure that standards are maintained and that customers, partners and the company itself are all protected. Domestic arrangements should also be in place to share information with law-enforcement agencies in different countries.

Where an organization experiences a fraud that is instigated from an overseas location, it should ideally be possible to trace the transaction, talk to the authorities in the other country and seek redress.

Foreign

Foreign jurisdictions represent the other side of the coin:

- If a fraudster is based abroad there may be a view that they are untouchable. They are able to be in contact with the victim company through Internet searches, email and even mobile phone.
- Company phones and laptops that contain personal data can be vulnerable to attack from a fraudster based abroad who succeeds in breaching security measures.
- Many domestic organizations trade with several different foreign entities, or simply allow overseas customers to transact with overseas companies' sales and information systems, thus providing an opportunity for fraud.

• Bribery is a major problem when companies do business abroad. The extra 'fees', 'local charges' and 'operating licences' that can be charged by foreign officials are often straightforward bribes that go into their pocket. The problem is that most developed countries have legislation that means that these types of bribe are illegal, even if undertaken unwittingly, and this could open the company to prosecution.

Countries that gain a reputation for being corrupt tend to find it hard to attract trading partners and often lose many would-be investors from around the world.

We need now to examine the three interfaces that can lead to fraud; that is, goods and services, financial data and issues relating to personal identity.

Goods and Services

Global consumer fraud works on several levels. A major threat is posed by website-based fraudulent traders who provide substandard goods, or no goods at all. Often they misrepresent their goods by one of the following:

• By claiming that the goods are genuine even though they are counterfeit.
• By boosting quality aspects that are not borne out in reality.
• By claiming that there is adequate after-sales care.
• By downplaying any drawbacks to their products and services.

Fraud Smart employees will do well to ensure that they protect their personal business transactions and look for signs that any of the above problems could arise when purchasing goods and services over the Internet.

Financial Data

Sophisticated foreign fraudsters can attack corporate databases and seek to secure financial data that they can use to commit fraud or simply sell on to the highest bidder. Note these points:

• The information security equation used to be just about protecting corporate IT facilities.

- With the advent of mobile computing it became about protecting corporate networks, company laptops and more recently staff mobile phones.
- Malware can be introduced into a victim's computer by creating a 'Trojan horse' that steals confidential information. This can be used by the hacker, for example, to transfer money from the victim's bank account to a temporary account that can be exploited by fraudsters.

With 'cloud computing' a company no longer needs to protect its internal systems, as all its data are held on remote servers that 'live in the clouds', without physical borders. Nevertheless, access to these huge databases of corporate information can be attempted by penetrating such 'clouds', which are maintained by specialist companies who act as third-party IT providers for their clients. In this environment security remains a key consideration.

Personal Identity

Cyber-fraudsters often focus on obtaining personal data to commit their frauds, using online penetration as their weapon of choice:

- Social networking sites have exploded over the last few years, particularly among the younger generation. If fraudsters can glean enough information about a victim, they can steal their identity and commit fraud in the name of the victim. If a consumer is using their pet's name or a family member's date of birth as security codes for their bank account, credit cards or other personal passwords, this information can be gleaned on social networks and used to breach passwords or access codes.
- Social networks allow individuals to connect with thousands of 'friends' across the world, and routinely exchange personal information on a real-time basis. Data privacy rules only work where information is given on the basis that it will be kept secure, and social networking can lead to private data being freely given out to people who purport to be trusted members of a social community, even though they may in reality be fraudsters.
- Privacy laws may be designed to protect those who reside in the country in question, not anyone who lives outside that country. Anyone who has access to an Internet service provider's database also has access to consumers' online browsing habits, which can be

mined and sold on to marketing companies, and there may in fact be no breach of privacy if customers are outside the domestic jurisdiction.
- A lack of privacy becomes all the more scary when it is possible to track private email exchanges, including those containing confidential details.

There is a clear link between terrorist activities and fraud. Identity fraud can be used to establish false identities for members of terrorist groups, while credit card, counterfeit goods and mortgage fraud are used to finance their activities.

Image Versus Reality

In the final analysis, the cyber-fraudster operates by creating an image that fits with whatever the victim wants to see, but does not reflect the reality of the situation:

- Fraudsters can cause tremendous damage to corporate reputations by hacking into a company's systems and then publicizing the breach. Alternatively, they can attack an IT system and threaten to continue their attacks unless they are paid off.
- As we have already said, malware can be planted into a system to disguise a fraudster's emails so that they appear to come from a reputable source. These emails can then be used for 'phishing', trying to obtain secure information from an individual by, say, asking for passwords as part of a bank's security checks.

In the virtual world, it can be very hard to decipher image from reality and it can sometimes be extremely difficult to distinguish between a genuine customer or partner and a complete fraud.

OUR THREE KEY CONCLUSIONS

Fraud is big business and there is definitely a growth in the number of criminal gangs and individuals who use the Internet to secure financial gain through their nefarious activities. As more and more people around the world are online, this threat can only increase.

There are three main conclusions that we can draw from our discussions and suggestions. These will be used to drive your Fraud Smart toolkit, which you will design at the end of this part of the book:

3.1 Cross-border fraud has to be addressed, since fraudsters exploit the power of the Internet along with their own specialist knowledge of weaknesses in corporate security measures to commit cyber-fraud.
3.2 The risks inherent in social networking sites and the way personal information is exchanged and stored should be fully appreciated if users are to protect themselves from fraud and abuse.
3.3 Online activity should be undertaken with care, since the image presented by the other party does not always fit the reality. Photos, personal details and even references can be manipulated to cloak fraudulent or deceitful behaviour.

It is important to adopt a stance that accepts that not everything we see and hear over the Internet can be trusted, even if it appears valid. In essence, global fraud is unacceptable behaviour masquerading as acceptable behaviour.

4
Building Your Fraud Smart Toolkit

We have looked at the concept of fraud at work and agreed that the only way forward is to involve everyone in the fight against employee fraud and abuse and the affects of organized criminal networks. As we have seen, this book is based around the Fraud Smart cycle, which covers five key aspects of helping non-specialists get to grips with fraud at work. This is repeated in Figure 4.1.

This chapter concludes the first part of the Fraud Smart cycle, Understanding the Threat, and covers the way in which you can think about building your own toolkit as a way of joining the fight against fraud.

KEY LEARNING OBJECTIVES

Let's return to the learning aims that were set for this part of the book:

To give you a good appreciation of the threat of fraud and its potential impact on an organization.

OUR FRAUD CYCLE

Mastering Suitable Controls

Understanding the Threat

Recognizing Red Flags

Appreciating Respective Roles

Embracing Sound Ethics

Figure 4.1   The Fraud Smart cycle.

This chapter gives you the chance to reflect on the key conclusions that have been developed in the chapters in this part of the book and how they can become part of your personal development strategy.

Key Conclusions	Personal Fraud Smart Toolkit
1.1 Fraud is ever present and is growing in most developed and emerging economies, so that it must be seen as representing a major threat to most organizations in most sectors.	Talk with your colleagues and find out whether they consider the possibility of internal and external fraud in their work area. Look for reports of employee fraud whenever you read your local and national newspapers. What type of common features do you see emerging from your reading? Make yourself aware of frauds that have occurred in organizations that bear similarities to your own employer. Is fraud seen as a major issue or just something that happens to other organizations? One interesting approach is to ask friends whether they know anyone who has been defrauded over the last few years. You also need to ask yourself whether you know enough about the threat of fraud to see it as a real issue.

(Continued)

Key Conclusions	Personal Fraud Smart Toolkit
1.2 It is no longer possible to sweep fraud under the carpet, hoping that any incidents can be dealt with by simply asking the culprit to resign.	Find out about your company's policy on prosecution for employees who attempt to defraud the employer. Have you come across any stories where 'bad apples' have simply left work under a cloud? Reflect on the implications of getting rid of dishonest people with no punishment or sanctions beyond asking the culprit to resign. Ask your colleagues if they have seen this happen in previous jobs.
1.3 Organizations own income, expenditure, assets and data and these are all at risk if there are no effective measures in place to ensure that everyone is Fraud Smart and is operating as a full-time custodian of the corporate resource.	Reflect on how fraud could happen in your organization in a way that affects: • Assets • Expenditure • Income • Data In what way could any of the above be at risk and is there a strong culture of protecting these resources in your work area? If you are able to think of any ways in which a culture can be encouraged where team members see themselves as custodians of company resources, discuss these ideas with your manager.
2.1 There is a wide range of potential deceptions that have to be addressed in the fight against fraud, ranging from financial misstatement and misappropriation through to bribery and corruption.	Executives have a duty to account for their activities and performance, but serious frauds may happen when these results are distorted. Are you able to demonstrate that the way in which your team report their results leads to a true and fair representation of these results and are there good controls in place to ensure that this happens?
2.2 The threat of fraud must be understood as ever present if it is to be tackled, and can be simple or complex depending on its nature and the way it is carried out.	Reflect on whether there are simple ways in which your colleagues could abuse their facilities or inflate their allowances as part of 'custom and practice'. Challenge yourself by accessing a few frauds reported in detail on the Internet. Follow the logic of these complex frauds and how they were perpetrated.

Key Conclusions	Personal Fraud Smart Toolkit
2.3 The fact that employees as well as outsiders can commit fraud should be fully recognized, in addition to the most dangerous scenario that occurs where the two groups conspire to act against a business.	Can you think of any ways in which a colleague could strike up an inappropriate relationship with an external party that may be used to defraud your employer, and what are the measures to guard against this risk? Also discuss how your colleagues relate to friends outside the workplace and whether they disclose details of their work to these social groups, particularly where they hold sensitive jobs. Reflect on the corporate protocols on personal contacts and company disclosures that might protect staff from criminal gangs seeking to exploit confidential information.
3.1 Cross-border fraud has to be addressed, since fraudsters exploit the power of the Internet along with their own specialist knowledge of weaknesses in corporate security measures to commit cyber-fraud.	Do some research into cyber-fraud or people attempting to breach systems security to gain an illegal advantage. Use your web browser to look at instances of cyber-fraud and some of the problems that this can produce. Have you uncovered any frauds that could hit your organization? Look at your government's published guidance on cyber-fraud and review the steps that are recommended to protect corporate and personal data. Ask yourself whether you know enough about this topic or if you need to find out some more.
3.2 The risks inherent in social networking sites and the way personal information is exchanged and stored should be fully appreciated if users are to protect themselves from fraud and abuse.	Talk to family and friends about their use of social networking sites and discuss any risks that arise from using these facilities. Pay particular attention to horror stories where problems have ensued and try to work out whether any of your friends made any mistakes that led to these problems. Make a list of ways to protect personal identity and financial data and talk about these measures with friends and family who may be exposed.

(*Continued*)

Key Conclusions	Personal Fraud Smart Toolkit
3.3 Online activity should be undertaken with care, since the image presented by the other party does not always fit the reality. Photos, personal details and even references can be manipulated to cloak fraudulent or deceitful behaviour.	Reflect on the people you do business with over the Internet and how you can be sure that they will provide goods and services to the agreed standards. Consider these security measures: • Web browser security settings. • Restricting the sharing of personal data. • Using up-to-date virus protection. • Only using secure payment systems. • Employing all available security tools provided by your bank for online banking. • Having a special bank account (with small balances) for online transactions or a top-up charge card. • Not storing passwords and excessive personal information on your laptop. • Using a laptop for online banking that does not contain contacts list, emails and personal data. • Destroying personal data when discarding a laptop. • Asking your bank to phone you to confirm spending on items over a set limit. • Checking all bank and credit card statements immediately they arrive. • Being careful when using public wi-fi connections. • Other recommendations by security specialists. Make an assumption that any person or business you deal with online may be a con artist and consider this a possibility until you can verify that all is well. Remember, the fraudsters will try to look and sound highly professional, but will want to hook you in with offers that sound too good to be true.

Consider building your Fraud Smart toolkit and decide if any of the above tasks should be incorporated into your personal development plan that you agree with your boss. Now have a go at the multichoice quiz for Part I of the book, check your answers against Appendix B and record your score in Appendix C.

PART I MULTICHOICE QUIZ

1 Insert the missing words.
   The threat of fraud has grown not only due to the economic downturn but also because . . . .
   . . . . have been removed, and low-paid junior staff now have much more responsibility, including instant access to customer information as online commerce becomes the norm.
   a staff bonuses
   b management layers
   c performance targets
   d suspect behaviour

2 Which is the most appropriate statement?
   a Fraud is any intentional act or omission designed to deceive others, resulting in the victim suffering a loss and/or the perpetrator achieving a gain.
   b Fraud is any unintentional act or omission designed to deceive others, resulting in the victim suffering a loss and/or the perpetrator achieving a gain.
   c Fraud is any intentional act designed to deceive others, resulting in the victim suffering a loss and/or the perpetrator achieving a gain.
   d Fraud is any intentional act or omission designed to deceive others, resulting in the victim suffering a loss and the perpetrator achieving a gain.

3 Insert the missing words.
   Fraud is not. . . . . It is unfair, as it diverts funds from the people and entities that have a legal right to those funds.

a harmless, victimless and therefore of some concern
b significant, victimless and therefore of low concern
c harmless, victimless and therefore of low concern
d harmless, victimless, non-violent and therefore of low concern

4 Insert the missing words:
Our model suggests that we can view fraud as affecting at least four main aspects of an organization, that is . . . .
. . . .
a its income received, its spending, its data (or information) and its staff.
b its income received, its cash, its data (or information) and its assets.
c its income received, its spending, its data (or databases) and its assets.
d its income received, its spending, its data (or information) and its assets.

5 Which is the least appropriate statement?
There are several questions that can be asked to assess how expenditure could be at risk, including for example:
a Could someone boast about their achievements and thereby earn more money than they otherwise should have?
b Could someone falsify their timesheet, overtime claim, expenses or performance figures to earn extra income?
c Could a fabricated order be placed that leads to a fraudulent payment being generated?
d Could duplicate payments be scheduled and one of the duplicates then diverted?

6 Which is the most appropriate statement?
a Fraud is ever present and growing in most developed and emerging economies, such that it must be seen as representing a major threat to some organizations in some sectors.
b Fraud is ever present and growing in several developed and emerging economies, such that it must be seen as representing a major threat to most organizations in most sectors.
c Fraud is ever present and growing in most developed and emerging economies, such that it must be seen as representing a major threat to most organizations in most sectors.

d Fraud is ever present and slowing down in most developed and emerging economies, such that it must be seen as representing a major threat to most organizations in most sectors.

7 Insert the missing words.
Protecting income, expenditure, assets and data is, in the end, about protecting the . . . . of an organization.
a management
b executives
c goods
d reputation

8 Insert the missing words.
. . . . are disproportionately victimized by occupational fraud. These organizations are typically lacking in anti-fraud controls compared to their larger counterparts, which makes them particularly vulnerable to fraud. (ACFE Report, page 4)
a All organizations
b Small organizations
c Larger organizations
d Public-sector bodies

9 Which is the most appropriate statement?
a We are most concerned in this book with international fraud, which is about dishonestly using one's occupation for personal gain.
b We are most concerned in this book with employee fraud, which is about dishonestly using one's knowledge for personal gain.
c We are most concerned in this book with employee fraud, which is about dishonestly using one's occupation for virtual gain.
d We are most concerned in this book with employee fraud, which is about dishonestly using one's occupation for personal gain.

10 Which is the least appropriate statement?
Corruption includes:
a bribery and gratuities to companies, private individuals or public officials.
b receipt of bribes, kickbacks and gratuities.
c theft of equipment
d aiding and abetting fraud by other parties (e.g. customers, vendors).

11 Insert the missing words.
   It is simply the case that . . . . could undermine a
   business relationship. We need to be aware that occasionally people
   succumb to temptation, and that some do so more readily than
   others.
   a stress
   b ethics
   c deceit
   d aggression

12 Insert the missing words.
   The best frauds, from the fraudster's point of view, are those that
   are . . . . and remain hidden for many years. The next
   best are those that should never have happened, and if revealed
   would embarrass the managers or even lead to charges of neglect.
   a not detected
   b small in size
   c large
   d smash and grab

13 Which is the most appropriate statement?
   a Some complex frauds can be carefully planned, where a fraudster
     will engage in a series of banking transfers over many months
     so that this pattern is used to counter controls that are activated
     for regular transactions.
   b Some complex frauds can be unplanned, where a fraudster will
     engage in a series of banking transfers over many months so that
     this pattern is used to counter controls that are activated for
     suspect transactions.
   c Some complex frauds can be carefully planned, where a fraudster
     will engage in a series of banking transfers over many months
     so that this pattern is used to activate controls that are activated
     for suspect transactions.
   d Some complex frauds can be carefully planned, where a fraudster
     will engage in a series of banking transfers over many months
     so that this pattern is used to counter controls that are activated
     for suspect transactions.

14 Insert the missing words.
   In fact, some professional criminals . . . . into
   financial services companies to allow them to understand and get

around controls that are meant to protect against these criminal activities.

a go online
b plant employees
c do academic research
d place adverts

15. Insert the missing word.
Most . . . . are loath to abide by rules created by other jurisdictions and there may well be some friction between countries that are not used to cooperating with each other.
a jurisdictions
b dictators
c auditors
d lawyers

16 Which is the most appropriate paragraph?
  a Occupational fraud is a global problem. Though some of our findings differ slightly from region to region, most of the trends in fraud schemes, perpetrator characteristics and anti-fraud controls are not similar regardless of where the fraud occurred.
  b Occupational fraud is a local problem. Though some of our findings differ slightly from region to region, most of the trends in fraud schemes, perpetrator characteristics and anti-fraud controls are similar regardless of where the fraud occurred.
  c Occupational fraud is a global problem. Though some of our findings differ slightly from region to region, most of the trends in fraud schemes, perpetrator characteristics and anti-fraud controls are similar regardless of where the fraud occurred.
  d Occupational fraud is a global problem. Though some of our findings differ slightly from region to region, most of the trends in fraud schemes, perpetrator dress styles and anti-fraud controls are similar regardless of where the fraud occurred.

17 Which is the least appropriate statement?
Each country that trades internationally needs to have its own domestic arrangements to protect customers wherever they reside:
  a They will also need a set of protocols to deal with frauds that cross national borders and continents.
  b Each country should align its judicial and legal systems with other countries.

c In fact, many companies have bases in different countries around the world and there needs to be collaboration to ensure that standards are maintained and that customers, partners and the company itself are protected.

d Domestic arrangements should also be in place to share information with law-enforcement agencies in different countries.

18 Which is the most appropriate statement?
a We now need to examine the three interfaces that can lead to fraud; that is, goods and commodities, financial data and issues relating to personal identity.
b We now need to examine the three interfaces that can lead to fraud; that is, goods and services, financial data and issues relating to personal ability.
c We now need to examine the three interfaces that can lead to fraud; that is, goods and services, financial data and issues relating to personal identity.
d We now need to examine the three interfaces that can lead to fraud; that is, personal services, financial data and issues relating to personal identity.

19 Insert the missing words.
Countries that gain a reputation for being . . . . tend to find it hard to attract trading partners and often lose many would-be investors from around the world.
a very corrupt
b very ethical
c serious about fraud
d hard-working

20 Which is the least appropriate statement?
Global consumer fraud works on several levels. A major threat involves website-based fraudulent traders who provide substandard goods, or no goods at all. Often they misrepresent their goods by:
a claiming they are genuine when they are counterfeit.
b boosting quality aspects that are not borne out in reality.
c making it clear that there is no after-sales care.
d downplaying any drawbacks from their products and services.

PART II
Appreciating Respective Roles

Learning Objective

> *To help you appreciate your role in fraud control and the need to discharge this role by being Fraud Smart.*

5
Fraud Smart Roles and Responsibilities

In the first part of the Fraud Smart cycle we established that there is a worrying threat of fraud that needs to be addressed and that we all have a role in this matter. Let's take another look at the Fraud Smart cycle, which covers five key aspects of helping non-specialists get to grips with fraud at work. This is repeated in Figure 5.1.

This chapter sits within the second part of the Fraud Smart cycle, Appreciating Respective Roles, and covers the need to appreciate our role and that of others in responding to the threat of fraud.

WHAT CAN GO WRONG?

It is just not good enough to employ people and put them to work without thinking through the damage they could do if they were dishonest. Frauds happen when controls fail and someone takes advantage of a situation in which no one bothers to raise concerns about poor controls.

We can consider the way problems are able to arise by looking at two brief illustrative case studies taken from the UK and the USA. The first involved an IT company.

Figure 5.1   The Fraud Smart cycle.

CASE STUDY

A company director says that he was nearly forced to lay off staff after being ripped off by one of his salesmen. Extra checks have now been put in place to ensure that the company is never defrauded again, after one of its salesmen pleaded guilty to 12 counts of fraud, one charge of theft and one of abuse of position. He was given an eight-month prison sentence suspended for two years and ordered to carry out 120 hours of compulsory unpaid work along with a confiscation order for £9674.

The company has been going for 40 years and the salesman had been with it for three years, being described as 'a very high-achieving sales guy'. The company specializes in finding IT contractors who go out and work on client sites and the fraud was carried out by putting deals into the system that were completely false. The company spokesperson said, 'Because he'd been here three years and had been working well, we had no reason to worry. He was very convincing and we had no reason to doubt his contracts were genuine. It's not unusual for us to be paid further down the line and the salesman to get his commission. Now we don't take anything at face value. We were walking around last year thinking things were looking good because we'd got £90 000 coming in. We thought we were doing OK. The company has now introduced additional verification checks on sales and we do not pay people unless we see actual sales details.'

Those responsible for checking staff claims need to ensure that these claims are accurate.

CASE STUDY

A senior Chief Medical Laboratory scientific officer was sentenced to 12 months' imprisonment for defrauding a hospital of over £17 000. The laboratory officer falsified travel expense claims over several years, saying that he was visiting suppliers to view equipment when he was actually making personal journeys or none at all. The case was investigated by the anti-fraud team after colleagues raised concerns. He pleaded guilty to seven charges of false accounting, paid back £17 700 and resigned from his post.

WHAT DO THE EXPERTS SAY?

The first of our comments from our two key texts makes it clear that an organization cannot sit back, as tended to be the case in days gone by, and simply rely on its auditors to prevent and detect fraud as their prime role:

> Organizations tend to over-rely on audits. External audits were the control mechanism most widely used by the victims in our survey, but they ranked comparatively poorly in both detecting fraud and limiting losses due to fraud. Audits are clearly important and can have a strong preventative effect on fraudulent behavior, but they should not be relied upon exclusively for fraud detection. (ACFE Report, page 5)

So who should protect an organization against fraud? As with all good corporate policies, the drivers should sit right at the top of the business; that is, with the board of directors:

Reactions to recent corporate scandals have led the public and stakeholders to expect organizations to take a 'no fraud tolerance' attitude. Good governance principles demand that an organization's board of directors, or equivalent oversight body, ensure overall high ethical behavior in the organization, regardless of its status as public, private, government, or not-for-profit; its relative size; or its industry. (MBRF, page 5)

All organizations need good governance, in the sense that those at the top represent the best interests of the stakeholders and are able to drive this concept down through the business. In terms of fraud control, they set the tone, they prepare the anti-fraud policy, they approve the fraud-control strategy and they ensure that these are put into place to minimize fraud. But that is not the end of the matter. The board of directors is supposed to set a zero-tolerance tone, particularly when it comes to any unacceptable behaviour from top managers:

The board's role is critically important because historically most major frauds are perpetrated by senior management in collusion with other employees. Vigilant handling of fraud cases within an organization sends clear signals to the public, stakeholders, and regulators about the board and management's attitude toward fraud risks and about the organization's fraud risk tolerance. (MBRF, page 5)

The experts say quite clearly that we are all in the front line of fraud control and this is the premise on which this book is based:

In addition to the board, personnel at all levels of the organization – including every level of management, staff, and internal auditors, as well as the organization's external auditors – have responsibility for dealing with fraud risk. Particularly, they are expected to explain how the organization is responding to heightened regulations, as well as public and stakeholder scrutiny; what form of fraud risk management program the organization has in place; how it identifies fraud risks; what it is doing to better prevent fraud, or at least detect it sooner; and what process is in place to investigate fraud and take corrective action. (MBRF, page 5)

The board should ensure that fraud is kept on its agenda. One way of doing this is to assign responsibility for fraud risk management to a designated board member. The board may also assign an oversight role to a committee to ensure that the issue is not lost in the thrust of urgent board business. In many organizations this may be a specialist forum that looks at fraud oversight or more often the task is given to the audit committee:

> The audit committee should be composed of independent board members and should have at least one financial expert, preferably with an accounting background. The committee should meet frequently enough, for long enough periods, and with sufficient preparation to adequately assess and respond to the risk of fraud, especially management fraud, because such fraud typically involves override of the organization's internal controls. It is key that the audit committee receive regular reports on the status of reported or alleged fraud. (MBRF, page 12)

The audit committee will be able to consider the work of the external auditors as they review the financial statements and then make sure any inconsistencies are fully resolved. They will also receive reports from the internal auditors, who will be fully aware of the risk of fraud and will always probe suspicious items that they come across during the course of their audit work. Like the external auditor, internal audit's primary role is not to detect fraud. Internal audit can, however, be asked to carry out regular reviews of the way fraud risk management is undertaken and report this back to senior management and the audit committee.

Many larger organizations have established specialist fraud teams that have a remit to look for fraud and carefully investigate any suspected or actual frauds on behalf of a senior manager, while the legal team and human resources staff will tend to provide ongoing advice when an employee is being investigated. However, in addressing fraud control managers have the key role and this should be enshrined in their job descriptions and ongoing performance appraisal schemes. Managers can only succeed through the efforts of their staff; that is, the entire workforce.

Our final word from the experts is to reinforce the role of all levels of staff, including management, who should:

- Have a basic understanding of fraud and be aware of the red flags.
- Understand their roles within the internal control framework. Staff members should understand how their job procedures are designed to manage fraud risks and when noncompliance may create an opportunity for fraud to occur or go undetected.

- Read and understand policies and procedures (e.g. the fraud policy, code of conduct, and whistleblower policy), as well as other operational policies and procedures, such as procurement manuals.
- As required, participate in the process of creating a strong control environment and designing and implementing fraud control activities, as well as participate in monitoring activities.
- Report suspicions or incidences of fraud.
- Cooperate in investigations. (MBRF, page 14)

OUR MODEL EXPLAINED

We have developed a simple model in Figure 5.2 to illustrate one way of dealing with the issues raised in this chapter.

Our model puts *you* right at the top. It suggests that everyone, including non-specialists, needs to have some knowledge of the anti-fraud policy, fraud prevention, fraud detection and also how to respond if a fraud is suspected in the workplace. This concept should also apply

Figure 5.2   Anti-fraud roles.

to partners, agents, consultants, associates, contractors, key suppliers and anyone who has a close working relationship with the organization.

We can explore these issues by considering each separate part of our model in turn.

Corporate Anti-Fraud Policy

The entire workforce should be aware of the anti-fraud policy and should be able to appreciate its importance and comply with its provisions. Most policies cover the basic high-level sentiments for promoting fraud control and should address questions such as:

- What is fraud?
- Why does it pose a threat to all organizations?
- What do our values and ethics say?
- What roles do we have in fraud control?
- How do you help prevent fraud at work?
- How do you report suspicious circumstances?
- What is our stance on discipline and prosecution?
- What is available in terms of fraud awareness training?
- Where can you find the anti-fraud strategy?
- Where can you go for further information?

Each employee and associate should be able to answer these and other related questions to be an effective deterrent against fraud and corruption at work. Note that a Fraud Smart Policy is included as Appendix A of this book.

Fraud Prevention

As well as a good knowledge of the anti-fraud policy, each employee should appreciate how good controls can act as a safeguard against the risk of fraud:

- This includes the need to understand and comply with existing controls that protect resources and ensure that no one person has too much control over sensitive parts of the business. Controls ensuring that transactions are properly approved and that audit trails record who did what are also important.

- The new-look organization means that front-line staff tend to be the face of the business and have access to all the information and resources they need to get the job done. Business works on a real-time basis and many companies and service outfits have to act quickly to win business and please the customer. There is often very little time to spend on verification and checking routines to make sure that all transactions are valid. In this environment, it is necessary to operate sound controls to keep sight of the need to address the threat of fraud.

In terms of respective roles, everyone should know the basics of internal control and the need to tighten controls for high-risk transactions and in high-risk environments. Nothing less than that is acceptable.

Fraud Detection

Where controls fail, fraud may happen. Even when good controls are in place, a canny employee can work out ways of getting around them to access assets that should have been protected:

- A manager and a team member may conspire and fabricate an entire set of documents to steal from their employer. Anything can happen where there is a will and knowledge held by a crooked employee.
- The workforce should be aware that this can happen and should know how to be alert to the possibility of an opportunist crime or of ongoing scams. This means that managers, supervisors, work teams and front-line agents should be able to spot a fraud that either is obvious or raises inconsistencies that need to be probed.
- Detection tends to happen when two and two add up to three and questions are asked. Many frauds that come to light are greeted with the view that staff knew something was wrong but did not think it could relate to fraud. In fact, some frauds start with an employee making a mistake and realizing that no one picks it up. As they go on to repeat this action and remain undetected, they push forwards and commit major acts of misappropriation, knowing that they will not be found out.

Alert staff who follow up on odd mistakes or unusual incidents can act as a major control in stopping frauds at an early stage or even ensuring that they are not undertaken at all. Complaints can be a major source of identifying irregularities. A complaint may result from a basic error, staff incompetence or some form of misunderstanding that has led to the problem. However, after having looked into all these possible causes, a Fraud Smart employee may need to consider the possibility of internal fraud that has led to the discrepancy or anomaly.

Fraud Response

The final aspect of the workforce's role in fraud control relates to responding to frauds once they have been detected:

- Fans of crime thrillers may be tempted to plunge themselves into an exciting set of circumstances when they become aware that someone close to them is up to no good. For instance, they might check what is on the suspect's computer or go through their personal possessions in a desk or company locker, or they might discuss the person's possible guilt with a mutual friend. All of those are the wrong actions.
- If someone boots up the computer of a suspected fraudster, they become the last person to activate the computer. This fact may undermine a future prosecution that depends on what files the defendant had accessed on their work computer.
- If the suspect's personal possessions are searched, it may infringe crucial privacy rules that operate in that part of the world or in that particular organization and again may undermine management's response to the allegations and taint anything found in the search.
- If the case is discussed with a friend, it may become defamation in seeking to damage the reputation of the suspect based on unsubstantiated allegations or suspicions.
- As such, it is important that we all know how to respond to an actual or suspected fraud. In most cases, the response may be to inform an immediate line manager. Failing that, inform an authorized party, such as internal audit or human resources, depending on the corporate anti-fraud policy. For more senior employees, some knowledge of the way frauds are investigated may also be required, as the investigators may require cooperation and assistance as they search for and review the available evidence.
- One other consideration is that control weaknesses need to be closed when a fraud is discovered and this will be another part of the fraud response strategy. There may be a requirement for a quick fix, in terms of freezing certain accounts or changing access facilities to

particular systems. There will also be a planned response to tighten up controls as part of a longer-term solution.

Once again, Fraud Smart employees should be prepared to get involved in responding to an allegation of fraud and correcting any poor controls in areas for which they are responsible.

OUR THREE KEY CONCLUSIONS

It is a good idea to set clear roles and responsibilities within the anti-fraud policy so that everyone knows where they fit in. Once these roles are clarified, people should be made aware of them and, more importantly, equipped to discharge their duties in a competent way.

We have dealt with this basic concept in this chapter and there are three main conclusions that we can draw from our discussions and suggestions. These conclusions will be used to drive your Fraud Smart toolkit, which you will be designing at the end of this part of the book:

5.1 The corporate anti-fraud policy should document how the risk of fraud is managed and employees should be comfortable with their understanding of this policy.
5.2 Employees should be aware of the roles and responsibilities of the board, senior management and specialists in fraud control.
5.3 Employees should have a good understanding of their defined role in fraud control and also of the fact that any response to a fraud that has been uncovered should not infringe legal and regulatory protocols to avoid undermining the evidential basis of any ensuing investigation.

We said in the Preface that everyone who works for or is associated with a larger organization should appreciate what fraud is and its ramifications. It is not fair to make this statement without also making clear how people fit into how fraud is addressed, both as a risk and whenever it actually materializes. The onus is on the board of directors and the organization's management to ensure that this happens.

6
Fraud Smart Skills Profile

In the previous chapter we looked at roles and responsibilities in relation to preventing and dealing with fraud. Now we need to make sure that everyone possesses the right skills to discharge these additional duties at work.

As you know, this book is based around the Fraud Smart cycle, which covers five key aspects of helping non-specialists get to grips with fraud at work. It is repeated in Figure 6.1.

This chapter sits within the second part of the Fraud Smart cycle, Appreciating Respective Roles, and covers the need to ensure that the new-look employee has the right skill set to cope with the way fraud is carried out today.

WHAT CAN GO WRONG?

If we fail to live up to the expectation that the entire workforce is alert to the threat of fraud, much could go wrong. It is one thing to dictate new skills for employees, but quite another to ensure that these skills are firmly in place.

We can consider the way problems can arise by looking at two brief illustrative case studies taken from the UK and the USA. The first involved a huge fraud.

Figure 6.1   The Fraud Smart cycle.

CASE STUDY

A company director who defrauded a giant IT company by stealing
computer equipment was jailed for more than two years. The director
made 1200 claims for replacement parts to the company, over two
years, worth around £1.6 million. His assistant, who had worked
under him for eight years, copied the scam and used his own company
to defraud the employer of more than £80 000. The pair admitted
one count of fraud, which involved sending in parts that they
pretended were genuine parts within the warranty period and asking
for replacement parts. They knew that there was no way of knowing
whether the parts were within warranty or not. Different companies
were used for this scam. The judge said:

> Large companies who operate systems based on trust are just as
> entitled as anybody else to the protection of the law. This is a serious
> case of commercial dishonesty. You two between you were operating
> companies which sold parts. You hit upon this system of swindling
> your employer out of these various items. You were the effective
> brain and guiding hand in what went on over at least two years. It
> became clear that over a long period of time all was not right. There

> were well over 1200 claims by seven companies using something like 1100 different serial numbers to reclaim parts. The list price was in the region of £1.6 million overall. You are an intelligent man and have chosen a grossly inappropriate means of resolving a financial crisis.
>
> The director was sentenced to 32 months in jail, while his assistant received a nine-month sentence suspended for 12 months and was ordered to carry out 75 hours of unpaid work. Both were also banned from being a company director for five years.

Where controls are based on the view that all staff are always trustworthy at all times, unscrupulous individuals, particularly if they are in management positions, may seek to undermine the company. Fraud Smart skills mean being suspicious about transactions that do not add up:

CASE STUDY

A payroll officer was sentenced to 18 months' community service for paying herself more than £4000 to which she was not entitled. The officer used the payroll system to make payments to various bank accounts in her name for a year and then tried to cover up the offences by altering paperwork. After a manager at the hospital became suspicious and alerted the corporate fraud specialist, an investigation was carried out that revealed the improper payments. The payroll worker admitted two counts of false accounting with a further ten counts to be taken into consideration. She was also ordered to pay £4500 compensation.

WHAT DO THE EXPERTS SAY?

Our first reference from our two key texts suggests that at least one person at board level should have well-rounded expertise in fraud risk management, or at least be able to drive the anti-fraud policy into and down through the business:

The board should also monitor the organization's fraud risk management effectiveness, which should be a regular item on its agenda. To this end, the board should appoint one executive-level member of management to be responsible for coordinating fraud risk management and reporting to the board on the topic. (MBRF, page 7)

When there is a need to establish a full investigation of an alleged fraud, there is also a need to ensure that the team involved in the investigation possesses sufficient of the necessary skills. The next piece of guidance makes this point:

Depending on the specifics of the allegation, the investigation team may need to include members of different departments or disciplines to provide the knowledge and skill sets required. The following resources should be considered to determine whether their participation or assistance is necessary:

- Legal counsel.
- Fraud investigators.
- Internal auditors.
- External auditors.
- Accountants or forensic accountants.
- HR personnel.
- Security or loss prevention personnel.
- IT personnel.
- Computer forensics specialists.
- Management representative. (MBRF, page 41)

It is one thing to work out what skills the workforce need to engage fully in the fight against fraud, but there is a risk that the culture of the organization may encourage some agents to behave badly. Our final quote from the experts considers this problem:

HR managers should be involved in both the performance management and compensation programs. Performance management involves the evaluation of employee behavior and performance as well as work-related competence. It is a human trait to want recognition of competence and reward for positive performance and success. Regular and robust assessment of employee performance with timely and constructive feedback goes a long way to preventing potential problems. Employees who are not recognized for what they do and what they have accomplished, especially those who may have been bypassed for promotion, may feel their inappropriate and fraudulent conduct is justified. (MBRF, page 32)

OUR MODEL EXPLAINED

We have considered the skills base of the most senior person in charge of the anti-fraud policy and we have noted the need for sufficient skills in teams that get involved in fraud investigation. The skills required by the remainder of the workforce are discussed here.

We have developed a simple model in Figure 6.2 to illustrate one way of dealing with the issues raised in this chapter.

Our model suggests that solid fraud control involving all levels of employees will only work when the organization has identified what skills it needs for its workforce to become risk smart. We can explore these issues by considering each separate part of our model in turn.

Compliant

Every organization will set out its procedures and routines to ensure the smooth conduct of its business:

- These systems and controls will have emerged over many years and are designed to ensure that risk is minimized and corporate resources

Figure 6.2   The Fraud Smart skills profile.

are protected. A culture of complying with set controls is extremely important to ensure that staff will act in accordance with expectations.

- Anything less than this may open the door to problems such as identity theft and breach of data privacy or security. Now, more than ever before, each employee needs to appreciate the importance of complying with set procedures and that this is part of the organization's accepted culture.
- All developed countries have rules that protect against money laundering and identity theft, which often ask for rigid assessments to determine the true identity of customers before a high-value transaction is approved. Organizations should be aware of these and adhere to them.
- Good fraud prevention starts with staff who refuse to take shortcuts in the way they administer company procedures, bearing in mind that some external fraudsters can be quite convincing. There are many businesses that deal with large money transactions, such as banks, casinos, estate agencies, lawyers, accountants, bureaux de change and others, which can be targeted by fraudsters who want to launder funds.
- Moreover, regulatory regimes may fine companies that install unrealistic performance targets that encourage violation of company rules and lead only to short-term decisions.

One word of warning. While all staff should be compliant in adhering to procedures, there is always an overriding need for everyone to use their common sense to ensure that sticking to the rules does not also allow fraud to happen. Checking procedures are poor if they ask callers to verify their identity by referring to information that can be gleaned from a document that could have been stolen from the 'real' customer. In this case compliance will not always act as a reasonable control and a Fraud Smart staff member may want to do more. On the other hand, when there is a real emergency and someone's wellbeing is at risk if no action is taken, it may be necessary to navigate around the set procedures.

Being Fraud Smart is not about being suspicious of everyone and everything. It means being proactive in the way a set of circumstances are judged so that the organization's resources are always protected.

Honest

Is honesty a skill? And can it be learned? The answers to these two questions can appear vague when we try to deal with this rather opaque concept:

- An employer can check for dishonest behaviour by vetting criminal records before offering jobs to applicants. Drastic action can be taken where an employee has proved to be dishonest by lying or by acting in an unacceptable manner.
- What is more difficult is to teach employees to be honest and to make sure that this is part of their skills set. The only answer is to set high standards of conduct, make sure staff know what is expected of them and then monitor what goes on throughout the business.
- It is pretty much accepted that setting high standards is about having a good 'tone at the top', right from board level, and then driving this concept down into the organization through example and encouragement. The other necessity is to put in place clear sanctions where dishonesty is dealt with both firmly and quickly.

Bearing in mind the way zero tolerance is being applied to discourage dishonesty, everyone who works for an organization needs to ask themselves: Can I live up to these expectations and refuse ever to lie or act deceitfully, even if this means we may lose out on a business deal? The other side of the coin is for Fraud Smart people always to be prepared to challenge ambiguity or something that simply sounds wrong. Group think may pull team members in the same direction and team meetings may result in what the more outspoken members want. Nevertheless, every team needs to include people who question and challenge behaviour that is either suspect or could be seen as suspect by an outsider. Better still, all team members should have an inbuilt need to stick to the rules and play fair as part of the culture that is driven by the company's leaders.

Competent

Many frauds arise when employees operate within a chaotic environment where the rules are unclear and managers are not able to keep up with the demands of their job. As such, in order to promote an anti-fraud culture, staff need to be competent:

- The board of directors should possess the skills required to cope with the demands of a fast-changing business and live up to their duty to protect the corporate resource.
- Managers should be trained, qualified and able to understand the way controls guard against fraud and how these controls can be monitored. A worst-case scenario occurs when a manager suspects a fraud may be happening, but does not want this fact to come to light as it would expose failings in the way they have managed that part of the business. In this situation many organizations would revert to the old school of management that was discussed in Chapter 1, where dishonest employees would simply be asked to resign when they were eventually found out.

Competent employees are well placed to stand their ground when there is a chance that their work and decisions might be examined during any internal or external investigation.

Astute

Our final attribute is being astute. This simply means that every employee should have a really good understanding of the nature of fraud, the risk it poses and the way the organization faces this risk through its anti-fraud policy and resulting strategy:

- Customer-facing staff should know how to verify a customer's identity for normal business and even more so for high-value transactions. They should know how to protect corporate data and ensure that all access is correctly approved and applied in the correct manner.
- They should understand the dangers in altering client data relating to name, address and bank account for any funds or goods that will be released by the organization.
- Astute people should ask lots of questions and know that custody of money, assets, funds and personal data should be verified through an audit trail and sufficient security.
- Moreover, astute people should understand the dangers of talking in public and discussing confidential information at social events, particularly where alcohol is involved. The way processes are checked for reliability and integrity is a theme in how astute employees operate and they should not hesitate to sound an alarm when something suspicious comes across their desk. In one example a loans manager

reviewed an application for extended credit and wondered why the document was uncreased, when it should have arrived in a company envelope that necessitated its being folded. This simple deed led to further enquiries, which uncovered the fact that the document had been planted on the loans manager's desk by a fraudulent employee as part of a well-planned scam.

Being astute is about being judicious, being able to weigh things up and think them through in a fair and sensible manner. That is not to say that there is no room for the flair and high spirits that drive businesses to innovate and succeed. Being fair and judicious is not about winning at all costs, it is about playing by the rules.

OUR THREE KEY CONCLUSIONS

If, as we believe, all employees need to be part of the fight against fraud, then they should be equipped to be Fraud Smart or this strategy will fail. There are three main conclusions that we can draw from our discussions and suggestions in this chapter. These conclusions will be used to drive your Fraud Smart toolkit, which you will design at the end of this part of the book:

6.1 All organizations need to ensure that they do not operate an excessively pressurized performance culture that could undermine the personal integrity of their workforce by only focusing on short-term or shortcut goals.
6.2 All employees should act honestly and should at all times be able to comply with procedures and standards as a natural part of the way they perform at work.
6.3 All employees should be competent and astute in the way they work and appreciate that the risk of fraud sits alongside other, more common business risks that need to be addressed as part of the success criteria set by their employer.

We said in the Preface that everyone who works for or is associated with a larger organization should appreciate what fraud is and its ramifications. We need to make this ideal a reality by defining the skills necessary to meet this requirement and ensuring that employees either have these skills or are working towards them.

7
Fraud Smart Training Needs

The previous chapter identified the skills that are needed for fraud control. This chapter sets out a simple process for ensuring that these skills are in place.

As you know, this book is based around the Fraud Smart cycle, which covers five key aspects of helping non-specialists get to grips with fraud at work. This is repeated in Figure 7.1.

This chapter sits within the second part of the Fraud Smart cycle, Appreciating Respective Roles, and covers the way in which the right skills set can be secured.

WHAT CAN GO WRONG?

We know from the last chapter that the entire workforce should be compliant, honest, competent and astute. Having identified these skills, if we nevertheless fail to promote them properly, much could go wrong.

We can consider how problems can arise by looking at two brief illustrative case studies taken from the UK and the USA, at contrasting organizations.

Figure 7.1   The Fraud Smart cycle.

CASE STUDY

In 2006 the London regulator, the Financial Services Authority (FSA), fined a trading company (with a client base of 126 000 and funds under management of £9.8 billion) £300 000 for systems and control failings in breach of its principal businesses. The company became aware of fraud being perpetrated by a small number of its staff. Fraudulent payments of £328 241 had been made, in some instances to bank accounts held outside the UK. The criticisms levelled against the company were twofold:

- It had not carried out an adequate assessment of its fraud risk, in particular the risk of internal fraud. The FSA found that the firm should have taken a 'comprehensive approach' to identifying fraud risk before and after the discovery of the fraud and should have considered putting additional controls in place to mitigate any risks that were identified as a result of that review.
- Second, the firm's internal controls were found to be deficient, particularly in respect of ensuring that requests for changes to

client data and payment instructions were genuine and the lack of effective training given to staff to raise awareness of fraud risk. The FSA was particularly concerned that, had clients not queried the fraudulent transfers from their holdings, there was a material risk that the fraud would have continued.

Where there is a lack of good training, there will be gaps in the skills and knowledge that are needed to understand fraud, design effective controls and keep these controls under review. Poor training can result in poor staff, which can mean business failure, losses and even fines. Where those responsible for operating controls and supervising staff have no real awareness of employee fraud risks, there is no driver for ensuring that controls guarding against fraud are in place and applied:

CASE STUDY

After entering guilty pleas to three felony theft charges and one misdemeanour, a former volunteer cub scout treasurer received a sentence of 45 days in jail and 100 hours of community service for stealing more than $4000 from a cub scout pack's funds. An investigation revealed that these thefts started in 2008, only a few months after the defendant began volunteering for the scouts as their treasurer. Furthermore, according to court documents, the defendant's purpose was to deprive the cub scout pack of their funds by writing cheques made out to cash and cashing them at local banks in three towns. The thefts continued for four months until the scout pack's leader discovered money missing from a current account.

WHAT DO THE EXPERTS SAY?

For those who question the need to invest in staff fraud awareness training, we can turn to our two key texts for a warning about the impact of fraud in terms of increasing regulation:

> Regulations such as the U.S. Foreign Corrupt Practices Act of 1977 (FCPA), the 1997 Organization for Economic Co-operation and Development Anti-Bribery Convention, the U.S. Sarbanes-Oxley Act of 2002,

the U.S. Federal Sentencing Guidelines of 2005, and similar legislation throughout the world have increased management's responsibility for fraud risk management. (MBRF, page 5)

While a company can be fined if it does not sort out its fraud control arrangements, it is the managers who must be held accountable for making sure that fraud control works at ground level:

> The laws of most countries prohibit theft, corruption, and financial statement fraud. Government regulations worldwide have increased criminal penalties that can be levied against companies and individuals who participate in fraud schemes at the corporate level, and civil settlements brought by shareholders of public companies or lenders have rocketed to record amounts. Market capitalizations of public companies drop dramatically at any hint of financial scandal, and likewise, customers punish those firms whose reputations are sullied by indications of harmful behavior. Therefore, it should be clear that organizations need to respond to such expectations, and that the board and senior management will be held accountable for fraud. In many organizations this is managed as part of corporate governance through entity-level controls, including a fraud risk management program, (MBRF, page 11)

Our final quote reinforces the need to secure a budget for anti-fraud programmes:

> The board may choose to delegate oversight of some or all of such responsibilities to a committee of the board. These responsibilities should be documented in the board and applicable committee charters. The board should ensure it has sufficient resources of its own and approve sufficient resources in the budget and long-range plans to enable the organization to achieve its fraud risk management objectives. (MBRF, page 12)

OUR MODEL EXPLAINED

We have developed a simple model in Figure 7.2 to illustrate one way of dealing with the issues raised in this chapter.

We have made it clear that training has to underpin corporate initiatives and the ensuing strategies. That is no less true for the anti-fraud provisions that all organizations should have in place. Where the workforce have the required skills to discharge their role, all is well. If

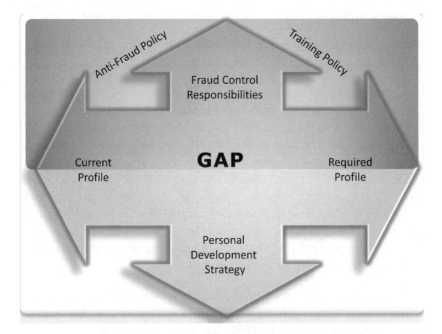

Figure 7.2 Fraud Smart personal development strategy.

not, the required skills will have to be acquired. Our model suggests that a process should be applied to get from point A, where you are, to point B, where you need to be. We can explore these issues by considering each separate part of the model in turn.

Anti-Fraud Policy

We have referred to this policy earlier in the book. It sets the scene for the entire personal development strategy that should emerge from our model:

- The policy lays out the aspiration of the board on the topic of combating fraud within the organization and how this will be organized, in outline.
- The anti-fraud strategy goes into much more detail and indicates how, over future periods, the threat of fraud will be addressed.

In fact, it should be possible to track the effects of the strategy down into the business through set objectives that will turn into clear actions that managers take to direct their resources towards business goals, and support the way the business is grown and kept safe.

Training Policy

Policies set standards, while there will also be strategies that assign resources to the right parts of the business:

- Corporate policies tend to call for higher levels of achievement and new or improved ways of doing things.
- These new directions, in turn, create the need for and inform the corporate staff training policy. When you want new or improved things to happen, staff need to be properly equipped to do them.
- The training policy will tend to say that staff will be developed in a way that ensures they are completely prepared to perform in a competent manner as well as being able to meet new challenges. In terms of the anti-fraud policy, the training policy will be geared around equipping the workforce to combat the threat of internal and external fraud by being Fraud Smart.

Because fraud and breaches of data privacy can occur from any part of the organization, from the mailroom to the boardroom, the training policy should be all-encompassing and reach every layer.

Fraud Control Responsibilities

We have to return to the previous chapter to reinforce the need to focus training on defined roles. The skills and attributes we have already discussed are:

- Compliant
- Honest
- Competent
- Astute

Employers will want to make sure their employees have these attributes, if the anti-fraud policy is to be fully implemented in creating a Fraud Smart workforce.

Current Versus Required Profile

This part of the process is quite straightforward. It means that each and every employee needs to perform a simple self-analysis, or in more rigid organizations where command-and-control regimes are in place the analysis may be something that is 'done' to staff. A simple table can be used to assist in this process:

Table 7.1 Anti-fraud attributes self-analysis.

Anti-fraud personal attributes	Desired level of knowledge and skills	Actual level of knowledge and skills	Personal development action required
COMPLIANT	1. Aware of all relevant policies and procedures. 2. Able to apply relevant operational procedures. 3. Understands compliance routines applied across the business lines.		
HONEST	1. Aware of all aspects of business ethics. 2. Able to reconcile tensions within ambiguous situations. 3. Provides leadership in ethical behaviour. 4. Able to challenge decisions that expose a conflict of interests.		
COMPETENT	1. Possesses the required knowledge, qualifications and experience for the job. 2. Undertakes training wherever appropriate. 3. Able to operate to high levels of performance. 4. Seeks to improve operations continuously.		
ASTUTE	1. Understands the nature of deceit and how it may manifest itself. 2. Able to negotiate around trusting people while also holding a healthy professional scepticism.		
OTHERS?	1. Understands the contents and guidance in this book.		

The idea is to set out the level of knowledge and skills required for each type of employee, as derived from the corporate anti-fraud strategy and the various suggestions in the table. Then use a variety of assessment measures agreed with line management to determine where you stand in contrast to where you should ideally be located. Assessments can involve whatever sources are agreed, such as personal judgement, colleagues' feedback (or that from peer groups), performance appraisal schemes, comments from customers and so on. The final stage is to list the actions needed to close the gap that has been defined through this analysis.

The 'honesty' attribute needs some commentary. Here we would ask Fraud Smart people to know the code of ethics, understand the sanctions and appreciate that there are ambiguous situations that are often hard to reconcile.

Personal Development Strategy

Our model suggests that the results that flow from the assessment process we have discussed will emerge as a personal development strategy. This strategy will form part of the normal business performance and development plan as a set of action points and measures that might be used to ensure each staff member is Fraud Smart and able to live up to the expectations in the corporate anti-fraud policy.

The key is to clarify what a Fraud Smart person will look like once they have acquired all they need to understand and to apply all the material and suggestions in this book as a minimum level of knowledge. Development then is all the steps that can be taken to become this Fraud Smart person over the next few months.

The analysis of current level of knowledge and skills against what should be in place can be used to set personal targets for closing any gap.

OUR THREE KEY CONCLUSIONS

There are three main conclusions that we can draw from our discussions and suggestions in this chapter. These conclusions will be used to drive your personal toolkit, which you will be designing at the end of this part of the book:

7.1 Employees should be in a position to know the standard of knowledge and skills required to live up to the expectations in the corporate anti-fraud policy.

7.2 All employees should take part in a process of analysing the extent to which these skills have been acquired and how far they need to be further developed.

7.3 Having identified any gap in existing skills, employees should be able to prepare a personal development strategy that seeks to close the gap.

All employees must know what is expected of them in terms of fraud awareness and to be able to acquire some personal development to help them live up to these expectations. Every organization will have its own interpretation of what being Fraud Smart means, and this book should be seen as the minimum level of basic and general knowledge that everyone should possess, whatever their official duties. Note that the chapters entitled 'Building Your Fraud Smart Toolkit', appearing at the end of each part of the book, may be used to help you with your Fraud Smart development strategy.

8
Building Your Fraud Smart Toolkit

In this part of the book we have looked at the fact that everyone within an organization has a defined set of roles and responsibilities that underpins the need to involve everyone in the fight against employee fraud and abuse and the activities of organized criminal networks. We can reiterate that this book is based around the Fraud Smart cycle, which covers five key aspects of helping non-specialists get to grips with fraud at work, as repeated in Figure 8.1.

This chapter sits within the second part of the Fraud Smart cycle, Appreciating Respective Roles, and considers the need to ensure everyone is able to fulfil their duties in conjunction with the corporate anti-fraud policy. Here we cover the task of helping you improve your personal Fraud Smart toolkit.

KEY LEARNING OBJECTIVES

Let's return to the learning objectives that were set for this part of the book:

To help you appreciate your role in fraud control and the need to discharge this role by being Fraud Smart.

OUR FRAUD CYCLE

Mastering Suitable Controls

Understanding the Threat

Recognizing Red Flags

Appreciating Respective Roles

Embracing Sound Ethics

Figure 8.1   The Fraud Smart cycle.

This chapter gives you the chance to reflect on the key conclusions that have been developed in the chapters in this part of the book and how they can become part of your personal development strategy.

Key Conclusions	Personal Fraud Smart Toolkit
5.1 The corporate anti-fraud policy should document how the risk of fraud is managed and employees should be comfortable with their understanding of this policy.	Have a look at your anti-fraud policy and make sure that you are familiar with its contents. Type 'anti-fraud policy' into a search engine and review some of the policies that are out there. Many companies attach an anti-fraud strategy to these policies as well. Test yourself – if someone asked you to describe your company's anti-fraud policy, would you be able to? If not, ask your boss how to remedy this gap. Being Fraud Smart starts with taking an interest in fraud and fraud control; it is not about ignoring the topic until it is forced on you. We must point to the age-old view that being proactive is better than simply being reactive.

(*Continued*)

Key Conclusions	Personal Fraud Smart Toolkit
5.2 Employees should be aware of the roles and responsibilities of the board, senior management and specialists in fraud control.	Ask your colleagues about their understanding of their role in respect of the anti-fraud policy and any fraud-control plan that covers your organization. Consider whether the answers fit with the guidance promoted in this book. If you feel that there are aspects of your role in fraud control about which you are unsure, research this issue with a view to closing the gap.
5.3 Employees should have a good understanding of their defined role in fraud control and also of the fact that any response to a fraud that has been uncovered should not infringe legal and regulatory protocols to avoid undermining the evidential basis of any ensuing investigation.	Ask your boss (or the person responsible for fraud investigations) how you should respond if you come across a fraud in your area of work. Make sure that you appreciate the importance of effective cooperation while not tainting any evidence with which you come into contact.
6.1 All organizations need to ensure that they do not operate an excessively pressurized performance culture that could undermine the personal integrity of their workforce by only focusing on short-term or shortcut goals.	Reflect on how performance is assessed in your work areas and whether this can lead to shortcuts or even low-level abuse by any of your colleagues. Business ethics is essentially about being fair, telling the truth and making sure that the customer's needs are met. This is a simple requirement that can be very hard for many enterprises to aspire to, when the competition seems to be using every trick in the book frantically chasing short-term sales. Talk to your boss about any concerns you may have in this respect.

Key Conclusions	Personal Fraud Smart Toolkit
6.2 All employees should act honestly and should at all times be able to comply with procedures and standards as a natural part of the way they perform at work.	Reflect on how honesty is defined at work and whether you have ever been in a position where your conduct may have been questionable. Think carefully about what helps you keep on the straight and narrow and how you can ensure you can never be accused of ambiguous or questionable conduct.
6.3 All employees should be competent and astute in the way they work and appreciate that the risk of fraud sits alongside other, more common business risks that need to be addressed as part of the success criteria set by their employer.	Reflect on the extent to which competence is defined in your organization and whether people take personal training and development seriously in making sure that they can live up to capability standards. Consider any steps you can take to improve your competence in performing at work, and make sure that your personal development plan is up to date.
7.1 Employees should be in a position to know the standard of knowledge and skills required to live up to the expectations in the corporate anti-fraud policy.	Have another look at your corporate anti-fraud policy and strategy and consider their contents carefully. Do you feel that your work team would benefit from additional training? If so, you might care to raise this matter with your manager. Remember that this book only contains a basic minimum for non-specialists and more detailed training will be required to fill any gaps.
7.2 All employees should take part in a process of analysing the extent to which these skills have been acquired and how far they need to be further developed.	Is there anything in the anti-fraud policy and strategy that you would like to explore further? If so, ask your boss whether you can talk to him or her or a fraud specialist for further guidance. The in-house experts will not mind talking to their colleagues across the organization if this will help the fight against fraud. They might even organize staff awareness events if asked.

(Continued)

Key Conclusions	Personal Fraud Smart Toolkit
7.3 Having identified any gap in existing skills, employees should be able to prepare a personal development strategy that seeks to close the gap.	Is there anything you could be doing to add to the tasks that are in your Fraud Smart personal toolkit? If so, talk to your boss and if appropriate go ahead and do it!

When building your Fraud Smart toolkit, decide whether any of the above tasks should be incorporated into your personal development plan that is agreed with your boss.

Now have a go at the multichoice quiz for Part II of the book, check your answers against Appendix B and record your score in Appendix C.

PART II MULTICHOICE QUIZ

21 Insert the missing words.
   Organizations tend to over-rely on . . . ., which was the control mechanism most widely used by the victims in our survey, but they ranked comparatively poorly in both detecting fraud and limiting losses due to fraud.
   a management control
   b external audits
   c company gossip
   d gut instinct

22 Insert the missing words.
   Good governance principles demand that an organization's . . . . .
   . . . ., or equivalent oversight body, ensure overall high ethical behaviour in the organization, regardless of its status as public, private, government or not-for-profit; its relative size; or its industry.

a management team
b stakeholder group
c fraud team
d board of directors

23 Which is the most appropriate statement?
   a The audit committee should meet frequently enough, for long enough periods and with sufficient preparation to adequately assess and respond to the risk of fraud, especially management fraud, because such fraud typically involves override of the organization's internal controls.
   b The audit committee should meet frequently enough, for long enough periods and with sufficient preparation to adequately assess and respond to the risk of fraud, especially management fraud, because such fraud typically involves override of the organization's internal audit.
   c The audit committee should meet frequently enough, for long enough periods and with sufficient preparation to adequately assess and respond to the risk of fraud, especially where criminal gangs are involved, because such fraud typically involves override of the organization's internal controls.
   d The trade union should meet frequently enough, for long enough periods and with sufficient preparation to adequately assess and respond to the risk of fraud, especially management fraud, because such fraud typically involves override of the organization's internal controls.

24 Insert the missing words.
   Like the external auditor, the internal audit's primary role is . . . .
   . . . . Internal audit can, however, be asked to carry out regular reviews of the way in which fraud risk management is undertaken and report this back to senior management and the audit committee.
   a to own fraud risk management
   b to assess staff performance
   c to detect fraud
   d not to detect fraud

25 Which is the least appropriate statement?
   Most anti-fraud policies cover the basic high-level sentiments for promoting fraud control and should address questions such as:

a What is fraud and why does it pose a threat to all organizations?
b What do your values and ethics say and what roles do you have in fraud control?
c How do you carry out covert surveillance?
d How do you help prevent fraud at work and how do you report suspicious circumstances?

26 Which is the most appropriate statement?
   a In terms of respective roles, team leaders should know the basics of internal control and the need to tighten controls for high-risk transactions and high-risk environments.
   b In terms of respective roles, everyone should know the basics of internal control and the need to tighten controls for high-risk transactions and high-risk environments.
   c In terms of respective roles, everyone should know about forensic science and the need to tighten controls for high-risk transactions and high-risk environments.
   d In terms of respective roles, managers should know the basics of internal control and the need to tighten controls for high-risk transactions and high-risk environments.

27 Insert the missing words.
   A complaint may be made by someone that results from basic error, staff incompetence or some form of misunderstanding that has led to the problem. But, after having looked into all these possible causes, a . . . . may need to consider the possibility of internal fraud that has led to the discrepancy or anomaly.
   a Fraud Smart employee
   b fraud specialist
   c senior manager
   d long-term customer

28 Insert the missing words.
   Where controls are based on the view that all staff are . . . .
   . . . ., unscrupulous individuals, particularly if they are in management positions, may seek to undermine the company.
   a sometimes trustworthy
   b fully trustworthy

c never trustworthy

d often incompetent

29 Which is the least appropriate statement?

  a HR managers should be involved in both performance management and compensation programmes.

  b Performance management involves the evaluation of employee behaviour and performance as well as work-related competence.

  c It is a human trait to want recognition of competence and reward for positive performance and success.

  d Regular and robust assessment of employee performance with aggressive feedback goes a long way towards preventing potential problems.

30 Which is the least appropriate statement?

Every organization will set out its procedures and routines to ensure the smooth conduct of its business:

  a These systems and controls will have emerged over many years and are designed to ensure that risk is minimized and corporate resources are protected.

  b A culture of complying with set controls is not really necessary to ensure that staff will act in accordance with expectations.

  c Non-compliance may open the door to problems such as identity theft and breach of data privacy or security.

  d Now, more than ever before, each employee needs to appreciate the importance of complying with set procedures and that this is part of the organization's accepted culture.

31 Insert the missing words.

All the people who work for an organization need to ask themselves, bearing in mind the way . . . . is being applied to discourage dishonesty, whether they can live up to these expectations and refuse to lie or act deceitfully, even if this means that they may lose out on a business deal.

  a compassionate tolerance

  b zero tolerance

  c risk assessment

  d staff supervision

32 Which is the least appropriate statement?
    As such, one more skill that is needed from staff who promote an
    anti-fraud culture is competence:
    a The board of directors should possess the skills required to cope
       with the demands of a fast-changing business and live up to their
       duty to protect the corporate resource.
    b Managers should be trained, qualified and again able to understand
       the way controls guard against fraud and how these controls can
       be monitored.
    c A worst-case scenario occurs when a manager suspects that a
       fraud may be happening, but does not want this fact to come to
       light as it would expose failings in the way they have managed
       that part of the business.
    d In this situation many organizations would revert to the old
       school of management, where dishonest employees would simply
       be prosecuted when they were eventually found out.

33 Insert the missing words.
    Being astute is about being judicious, which is about being able to
    weigh things up and think them through in a fair and sensible
    manner. That is not to say that there is no room for . . . .
    . . . . to drive businesses to innovate and succeed. Being fair
    and judicious is about winning, not at all costs but through playing
    by the rules.
    a cautious planning
    b tough controls
    c flair and high spirits
    d reckless adandonment

34 Insert the missing words.
    We know that the entire workforce should be . . . .
    . . . . Having identified these skills, if we fail to promote
    them properly, much could go wrong.
    a compliant, honest, sensible and astute
    b compliant, tough, competent and astute
    c compliant, honest, competent and astute
    d compliant, honest, competent and fair

35 Insert the two sets of missing words.
    Regulations such as the US . . . . ,
    the 1997 Organization for Economic Cooperation and Develop-

ment Anti-Bribery Convention, the US . . . . , the US Federal Sentencing Guidelines of 2005 and similar legislation throughout the world have increased management's responsibility for fraud risk management.

 a Foreign Corrupt Practices Act of 1977 (FCPA); Sarbanes-Oxley Act of 2002
 b Foreign Corrupt Practices Act of 1977 (FCPA); Sarbanes-Oxford Act of 2002
 c Foreign Corrupt Processes Act of 1977 (FCPA); Sarbanes-Oxley Act of 2002
 d Foreign Corrupt Practices Act of 1997 (FCPA); Sarbanes-Oxley Act of 2004

36 Which is the least appropriate statement?

 a We have made it clear that training has to underpin corporate initiatives and the ensuing strategies.
 b That is no less true for the anti-fraud provisions that all organizations should have in place.
 c Where the workforce have the required skills to discharge their role, then all is well.
 d If the workforce do not have the required skills to discharge their role, then the organization will have to be satisfied with the skills they do possess.

37 Which is the most appropriate statement?

 a In fact, it is impossible to track the effects of the anti-fraud strategy down into the business through set objectives that will turn into clear actions that managers take to direct their resources towards business goals, and support the way in which the business is grown and kept safe.
 b In fact, it should be possible to track the effects of the anti-fraud strategy down into the business through set objectives that will turn into clear actions that managers take to direct their resources towards business goals, and support the way in which the business is grown and kept safe.
 c In fact, it should be possible to track the effects of the anti-fraud strategy down into the business through set audit recommendations that will turn into clear actions that managers take to direct their resources towards business goals, and support the way in which the business is grown and kept safe.
 d In fact, it should be possible to track the effects of the anti-fraud strategy down into the business through set objectives that will

turn into clear actions that regulators take to direct their resources towards business goals, and support the way in which the business is grown and kept safe.

38 Which is the least appropriate statement?
Policies set standards, while strategies assign resources to the right parts of the business:
a These forces create tensions that tend to call for higher levels of achievements and new or improved ways of doing things.
b New or improved ways of doing things create the need for and inform the corporate staff fraud policy. When you want new or improved things to happen, staff need to be properly equipped to do them.
c The training policy will tend to say that staff will be developed in a way that ensures they are completely prepared to perform in a competent manner as well as being able to meet new challenges.
d In terms of the anti-fraud policy, the training policy will be geared around equipping the workforce to combat the threat of internal and external fraud by being Fraud Smart.

39 Insert the missing words.
When considering 'honesty', we would ask Fraud Smart people to know the . . . ., understand the sanctions and appreciate that there are ambiguous situations that are often hard to reconcile.
a rules of the game
b code of ethics
c personal targets
d poacher turned gamekeeper approach

40 Insert the missing word.
Our model suggests that the results that flow from the assessment process will emerge as a personal development strategy. This strategy will form part of the . . . . business performance and development plan as a set of action points and measures that might be used to ensure that each staff member is Fraud Smart and able to live up to the expectations in the corporate anti-fraud policy.
a normal
b additional
c executive's
d finance

PART III
Embracing Sound Ethics

Learning Objective

To give you an appreciation of the importance of ethical standards in fraud control and how these standards may be implemented.

9
The Moral Compass

We are now in Part III of the book, which is about embracing sound morals at work.

As you are aware, this book is based around the Fraud Smart cycle, which covers five key aspects of helping non-specialists get to grips with fraud at work. This is repeated in Figure 9.1.

This chapter sits within the third part of the Fraud Smart cycle, Embracing Sound Ethics, and covers the idea of a moral compass to point people in the right direction.

WHAT CAN GO WRONG?

Business ethics is much discussed as the straightforward concept of behaving honestly. But in truth, this idea of honesty can get very murky, as heightened competition calls for more and more aggressive behaviour and the workforce responds by doing everything they can to get a deal. At the same time, the idea of employee security has faded over the years as the corporate model moves away from long-term employment at the same organization to much shorter time frames, which creates a great strain on employee loyalty. If we fail to ensure that the entire workforce is firmly in touch with what the company is about, much could go wrong.

We can consider how problems can arise by looking at two brief illustrative case studies from the UK and the USA. The first is from the education sector.

Figure 9.1   The Fraud Smart cycle.

CASE STUDY

The reputation of a crucial government-backed league table was undermined after two senior lecturers were caught telling students to boost their college's rankings. The lecturers told their students that their degrees would be viewed as substandard by prospective employers if the university did not do well in the league tables. This national student survey was conducted as part of universities' quality assurance procedures.

There are many instances of fraud where the culprit has no qualms about obtaining benefits to which they have no moral right:

CASE STUDY

An accountant who defrauded over £10 000 from her employer was sentenced to 340 hours of community service. She gained substantially by altering a childcare register at a leading charity, with the result that she received the benefits of free childcare. The company operated a scheme where staff members could have childcare provided, with charges for this service being deducted from their monthly salaries. However, on 34 occasions, the accountant altered her details on the register or deleted them completely. After staff raised suspicions, she was fully investigated.

WHAT DO THE EXPERTS SAY?

Managing the Business Risk of Fraud contains extremely useful guidance on morals at work. One reference deals with the difficult issue of competing priorities, where the best interests of the employer may not sit alongside the best interests of an employee:

A process should be implemented for directors, employees, and contractors to internally self-disclose potential or actual conflicts of interest. Once conflicts are internally disclosed, there are several decision paths:
- Management may assert that there is, in fact, a conflict and require the individual to terminate the activity or leave the organization.
- Management may accept the internal disclosure and determine that there is no conflict of interest in the situation described.
- Management may decide that there is a potential for conflict of interest and may impose certain constraints on the individual to manage the identified risk and to ensure there is no opportunity for a conflict to arise. (MBRF, page 17)

It is important to deal with potential conflicts so that they do not put people in difficult situations:

The disclosure of a potential conflict of interest and management's decision should be documented and disclosed to legal counsel. Any constraints placed on the situation need to be monitored. For example, a buyer who has recently been hired in the purchasing department is responsible for all purchases in Division A. His brother has a local hardware store that supplies product to Division A. The buyer discloses the potential conflict of interest and is told that transactions with the hardware store are permitted, as long as the department supervisor monitors a monthly report of all activity with the hardware store to ensure the activity and price levels are reasonable and competitive. When the buyer is promoted or transferred, the constraints may be removed or altered. (MBRF, page 18)

OUR MODEL EXPLAINED

The concept of competing interests can undermine the moral compass. The compass sets a scope, width and breadth within which behaviour is deemed either acceptable or unacceptable, but this is put under strain when personal conflicts come into play.

We have developed a simple model in Figure 9.2 to illustrate one way of dealing with the issues raised in this chapter.

Our model suggests that, while the ethical direction of an entity can be set, people will tend to act in a way that satisfies their views on three key considerations: the employer's best interests, the wider society's interests and their personal best interests. That is, they should sit inside the middle of the model, where the question mark is. We can explore these issues further by considering each separate part of our model in turn.

Societal Best Interests

Most organizations have adopted a stakeholder view of business where the executives need to consider a range of interest groups, which

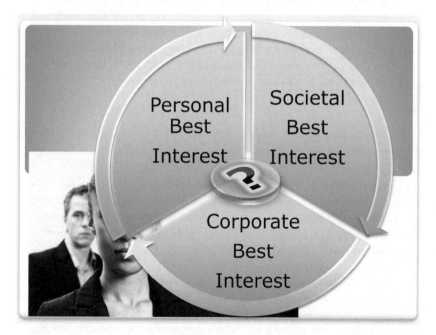

Figure 9.2   Conflicting interests.

together could be seen to represent 'society'. So the best interests of the wider society may have an impact on an organization and how its management behaves, which may include:

- Being environmentally conscious.
- Being fair to customers.
- Being fair to all employees.
- Protecting personal data that are held and not selling them on to marketing companies.
- Paying executive bonuses that are well earned and not disproportionate.
- Seeking to create long-term value that is sustainable.
- Being open and honest when dealing with shareholders and investors.
- Not exploiting labour in developing countries.
- Adhering to the law and best-practice concepts such as anti-bribery laws, anti-counterfeiting laws, policies on being fair to suppliers and considering the needs of local communities.
- Always living up to claims and representations that are made so that customers get a fair deal.

How far the above considerations are taken into account has an impact on the corporate reputation of the organization concerned, which in turn determines the degree to which the business or public service is trusted by actual or potential consumers. Any gaps in dealing with these attributes may cause public disquiet about the entity, which may mean that it falls behind the competition.

Organizations that work towards society's best interests will assume a good reputation, but it is often the case that, ironically, a less sincere and more aggressive business may be able to cut corners, be less than totally ethical and provide cheaper products that sell well as a result. We need next to consider the corporate best interests element to explore these issues.

Corporate Best Interests

A machine supervisor may refuse to operate a mechanical process that is used in the tobacco industry to produce more cigarettes for less money, on the basis that the product is not in society's best interests. However, this stance does not do much to promote the tobacco company's own best interests. An employee is under an obligation to work in the best interests of their employer. Where this falls outside the question mark in the middle of the model, there will be some conflict.

As another example, the corporate best interests of a large retail company may be to build as many out-of-town supermarkets as possible, but this new construction may damage local communities and wildlife. At the same time, the new development may bring in much-needed employment and create attractive shopping facilities for local people.

There will not always be a best fit between corporate and societal interests. The 2008 credit crunch is an example of what could go wrong, when finance companies went on a feeding frenzy to get excessive amounts of credit out to middle- and lower-income families.

Most organizations try to define their moral compass by setting out a code of ethics for their business that covers areas such as the following:

- *Integrity* – where the workforce and associates are expected to behave in an honest and fair way at all times.
- *Accountability* – where the entire workforce is expected to stand up and be counted for their actions, including any failure to act in safeguarding the business of which they are in charge.
- *Transparency* – where the business is run in a way that is open and clear, so that its activities can be appreciated by stakeholders and are not shrouded in mystery.

In the past, it was enough simply to prepare a code of ethics, but nowadays it is more important to demonstrate that employees are living up to a set of standards that meet the expectations of key stakeholders. Moreover, the idea is that corporate best interests should coincide as far as possible with society's best interests.

Personal Best Interests

In terms of the personal interests part of the moral compass, again the theory is quite simple, in that the workforce is asked to exhibit the behaviour that is defined in the corporate code of ethics. The difficulty lies on two levels:

- First, a manager or staffer can be tuned into the 'corporate best interests' but still commit fraud where parts of the business are suspect. For instance, a company may tell its sales staff to play up the benefits of its products and downplay the drawbacks, if the product is only suited to certain types of consumers. Strong sales may mean large profits and big sales bonuses. This may even mean that more tax is paid, which in a way does benefit society and may also promote local employment. The problem is that the practice may be bordering on fraudulent in terms of misselling and can implicate large parts of the workforce. So acting in the corporate best interests depends on whether the corporate body is itself acting in society's wider best interests.

• The second and more obvious problem occurs where an employee's personal best interests do not fully coincide with the employer's corporate interests. A sales consultant may organize their travel plans to maximize the expenses claim they later submit rather than maximizing the business opportunities for their employer. Another agent may monopolize a client with a view to taking them on, if and when they leave the company and go solo. It gets worse when this agent criticizes their employer and tells the client that they will be able to do much more when they become freelance. A final and more pointed example is where an employee acts in pursuit of their own interests by stealing from their employer because they have no interest in meeting the defined expectations of either society or the company.

The moral compass needs to have three dials: one pointing to society's best interests, one to corporate interests and another recognizing that people are motivated by what suits their own interests and encouraging movement to the middle ground that contains the question mark.

OUR THREE KEY CONCLUSIONS

Each organization has a moral compass that sets the direction for its entire workforce as a way of keeping them on the straight and narrow. In reality, the compass is not always able to keep still in turbulent times. In fact, it can alter depending on the angle at which it is viewed, which is why we argue that it needs three dials to keep in perfect balance.

There are three main conclusions that we can draw from our discussions and suggestions in this chapter. These conclusions will be used to drive your Fraud Smart toolkit, which you will design at the end of this part of the book.

9.1 The moral compass needs to be held steady to ensure that it balances the magnetic forces that may be in conflict and to avoid ending up off course.

9.2 The code of ethics should seek to reconcile the variables that underpin society's best interests and those of the organization in question.

9.3 Each employee should be given guidance and leadership to ensure that they are able to fit their personal interests into the dimensions created by the corporate code of ethics.

The moral compass that an organization establishes should create a mechanism for discouraging fraud and misconduct among its workforce.

10
Implementing Values

As we have already said, this book is based around the Fraud Smart cycle, which covers five key aspects of helping non-specialists get to grips with fraud at work. This is repeated in Figure 10.1.

This chapter sits within the third part of the Fraud Smart cycle, Embracing Sound Ethics, and covers the process of implementing values to help promote an honest workforce.

WHAT CAN GO WRONG?

Fraud is the result of deceit, which is the result of dishonesty. If efforts are directed at trying to get employees to rally round the concept of honesty and business ethics, there is a much better chance of preventing fraud among the workforce. It is one thing to prepare a code of ethics and statements about behaving fairly at work, but it is necessary to go further and implement these values across the organization. If we fail to do this, much could go wrong.

We can consider how problems can arise by looking at three brief illustrative case studies taken from the UK and the USA. Our first relates to a particularly sad example of a House of Lords peer (a law maker) in the British government, who was found guilty of making false expenses claims:

CASE STUDY

He said that it was 'common practice' for peers to claim the maximum possible in tax-free expenses in lieu of salary.

Figure 10.1   The Fraud Smart cycle.

This idea of 'common practice' was not accepted by the courts, but it is clear that if a culture of cutting corners appears in any walk of life, it can create blurred areas where ethics take a back seat. A more straightforward case illustrates what happens where there are no ethical dilemmas in play, just sheer greed:

CASE STUDY

A former chief executive was sentenced to 16 years in an American prison after pleading guilty to criminal charges over a scheme to hide the financial problems of his commodity brokerage. The judge accused him of arrogance, saying that he, like other white-collar defendants, often just didn't think that he would get caught. The prosecutors argued that he systematically lied about the company's financial condition in a scheme to inflate its value, sell his ownership interest and become rich.

Regardless of how many codes of ethics are in place within an organization, when the top people fail to abide by the values that underpin ethical behaviour, there is no scope for anti-fraud policies to work:

CASE STUDY

Three British directors of an American mining operation deliberately concealed their personal interest in a new share issue. Two of the men were board members of the mining company. Due to their professional involvement, they should have declared their personal stakes in the company when new shares were being issued on the London Stock Exchange, but they did not. The flotation was presented as a 'chance to strike gold'. A consultancy firm produced an attractive report on the company's prospects. However, the value of precious metals and base ore to be extracted from the company's mine workings were overvalued and the shares soon tumbled in price.

The gains made by the fraudsters out of the flotation, over £60 million, were hidden in an intricate network of offshore companies. This was only discovered during a raid on an accountancy firm in Jersey, in the Channel Islands. A joint investigation between the Serious Fraud Office and the City of London Police followed. The paper trail led investigators to Hong Kong, New Zealand, Monaco, France, Switzerland and Canada, as well as where the company was located in the USA, in order to unravel the ownership of a web of offshore companies. An 11-month trial finished with the conviction of three out of four men on charges of conspiracy to defraud in relation to the gold, silver, lead and zinc mining business.

WHAT DO THE EXPERTS SAY?

As one of our key texts notes, starting at the very top of the organization is normally a good idea:

> The board of directors should ensure that its own governance practices set the tone for fraud risk management and that management implements policies that encourage ethical behavior, including processes for employees, customers, vendors, and other third parties to report instances where those standards are not met. (MBRF, page 7)

The board of directors governs the business, applying the principles of corporate governance to ensure that stakeholders are treated fairly and that the organization is well run and controlled. Business ethics underpin this idea, although some argue that aggressive boards can be prompted by equally aggressive shareholders who search for short-term financial gains and are less interested in longer-term growth. That is why an appreciation of stakeholder theory is so important, to widen the business canvas and achieve the right corporate culture:

> Business stakeholders (e.g., shareholders, employees, customers, vendors, governmental entities, community organizations, and media) have raised the awareness and expectation of corporate behavior and corporate governance practices. Some organizations have developed corporate cultures that encompass strong board governance practices, including:
>
> * Board ownership of agendas and information flow.
> * Access to multiple layers of management and effective control of a whistleblower hotline.
> * Independent nomination processes.
> * Effective senior management team (including chief executive officer (CEO), chief financial officer, and chief operating officer) evaluations, performance management, compensation, and succession planning.
> * A code of conduct specific for senior management, in addition to the organization's code of conduct.
> * Strong emphasis on the board's own independent effectiveness and process through board evaluations, executive sessions, and active participation in oversight of strategic and risk mitigation efforts. (MBRF, page 10)

In the end, success in combating fraud comes back to business ethics and whether the culture is driven by an effective business ethics programme:

> Effective business ethics programs can serve as the foundation for preventing, detecting, and deterring fraudulent and criminal acts. An organization's ethical treatment of employees, customers, vendors, and other partners will influence those receiving such treatment. These ethics programs create an environment where making the right decision is implicit. (MBRF, page 11)

OUR MODEL EXPLAINED

In the previous chapter we introduced the moral compass. Here we talk about the way this compass has to be installed within an organization for it to be of any use.

Figure 10.2   Implementing business ethics.

We have developed a simple model in Figure 10.2 to illustrate one way of dealing with the issues raised in this chapter.

Our model suggests that while the code of ethics sets the direction through what can be a maze of contradictory paths, there are at least three ways to implement this direction in order for actions to sit within the culture of the organization. We can explore these issues by considering each separate part of our model in turn.

Corporate Code of Ethics

The code of ethics sets standards about expected behaviour and should address the usual areas such as integrity, accountability and transparency:

- It is about allowing the business to search for and create successful growth and also explore opportunities, but in a way that is fair and meets these expected standards of conduct. Since the code is for all employees, it should be set out in simple terms that capture the key messages the board wishes to deliver.

- At the same time, the code should be strong enough to deal with practical issues that face the type of business in question, such as bribery, corruption in overseas sites, employee share dealing (and insider trading), compliance issues or conflicts of interest when dealing with large contracts.
- The code should be designed so that it inspires the workforce to make the 'right' decisions even where there are some grey areas that are difficult to negotiate around. Where these decisions are too difficult, there should be access to ethical guidance.
- Where the codes are being misapplied, there should be an avenue for reporting unresolved ethical problems at work and outright breaches.

Pressure on corporate ethics tends to arise when a crisis occurs and there are different decisions to be made regarding whether to disclose all, compensate people, dismiss senior figures or simply keep everything low key. Some commentators argue that it should not take a disaster to work out what the code should say, since there may be a link to being fair in ensuring quality, safety and good risk management that should be part of the code of ethics in order to avoid foreseeable disasters in the first place.

Awareness

Once the code of ethics is in place, we need to tell everyone. The way in which awareness is managed gives a clue to how important the topic is seen to be at the top of the organization:

- All suitable measures should be employed to make sure that everyone knows about the code, it is fully understood and everyone is able to live up to its requirements.
- Posters, screensavers and regular mentions in staff communications can all be used to keep up the pressure on spreading awareness and making this a continuing process. For example, it is necessary to make clear on a regular basis how gifts and hospitality should be recorded in the relevant registers.
- To ensure that the code is designed and communicated well, ownership should be assigned at an early stage. The code could be driven by human resources, the legal department, the head of compliance or elsewhere so long as it has a boardroom sponsor.

- Awareness can be checked on a regular basis by carrying out annual staff surveys that assess the extent to which employees know and understand the code and whether it is applied in practice and promoted by senior management, including the infringement reporting line.
- The other approach is to get employees to sign that they have received the code and refresh their knowledge at least annually.
- Training is a major component of awareness and regular orientation and ongoing staff seminars should be run throughout the organization.

A code of ethics does not function as a code of ethics unless and until everyone knows about its content and is living up to the implied expectations. Being open and honest is not what people say they will do at work, it is more about what they do naturally according to their first instinct.

Disciplinary Code

This part of the implementation process is simply about ensuring that any breaches of the code are quickly investigated and dealt with under the disciplinary code of conduct:

- The need to discipline staff is the unfortunate result when the code has been infringed. Whenever there is an employee fraud, this will almost inevitably also mean that the disciplinary code of conduct has been infringed.
- Making discipline an important feature of resource management acts as a foundation for anti-fraud strategies. When an employee fraud has occurred, the disciplinary code must swing into action immediately. Even if a criminal conviction is not achieved at court (or even attempted), the employee in question can still be dismissed if they can be shown to have breached the disciplinary code of conduct.
- In terms of breaching company security, matters can become blurred when staff use social networking sites to comment on their employer or what they do at work. Many employers allow staff to access social networking sites and discussion groups as part of an enlightened management style, but there may be little regard to security issues and privacy among staff who place comments and information on public forums.

For complicated areas of work, it is a good idea to provide staff training events to make it clear what falls under the disciplinary code and what types of behaviour constitute a breach of the code. Fraud awareness training and business ethics courses should also cover the sad but real situation of what to do if and when things go wrong and disciplinary action has to be considered. It is only fair to tell people about corporate expectations and how seriously they are taken by the employer.

Assessment

The best way to implement business ethics is to keep assessing whether the efforts made so far have actually worked. There are several ways in which this can be done:

- Hold exit interviews with all leavers and ask whether there are any issues regarding business ethics that influenced their decision to leave, or whether there are any examples of inappropriate conduct that they wish to bring to management's attention.
- Conduct staff surveys as a useful way of measuring progress on making business ethics work.
- Report statistics on disciplinary issues and actual staff cases that have been heard each year or quarter.
- Ask the internal auditors to review the way in which the code of ethics is being applied within the organization and consider the results with care, particularly any areas for improvement suggested in the resulting recommendations.

The above may be put together to form what some call an ethical assurance process; that is, the process for ensuring that business ethics are making the right impact across the entire organization. It is better to have no code of ethics at all than to have one that does not go to the heart of how people behave at work.

Cultural Integration

The final part of our model relates to cultural integration. Ethics shoud be embedded inside the organization so that the workforce behaves well because they believe it is the right thing to do, rather than because they have been told to do so or risk getting sanctioned:

- This concept can operate at a high level. The so-called triple bottom line argues that corporate bodies should reach out to society and consider their *people* and how fair they are towards them; their *profits* and how far they have achieved their short-term targets; as well as longer-term sustainable growth and the impact of their activities on the *planet*.
- So business ethics sits within performance appraisal and stakeholder communications, as well as within the day-to-day decisions that are made across the organization.
- Many organizations develop compliance programmes where they check that employees are following the law and also working within the spirit of appropriate legislation and regulations. Ignorance of the law is no excuse; penalties and fines could result when employees within an organization engage in activities that violate relevant laws.

Every time an employee attempts to defraud their employer or seeks to use their employment for illegal gain, we can say that the code of ethics has failed to reach this person. That means that every time an internal fraud occurs we should ask: What went wrong with our values and how did a member of our corporate family slip through the net? The greatest bond that holds a workforce together is the fear of letting down their friends and colleagues. Employee fraud happens when this bond is either broken or the managers did not bother to give the encouragement and support needed to build it in the first place. The only exception to the argument is the rare but sometimes found fraud psychopath, who is unable to truly bond with anyone.

OUR THREE KEY CONCLUSIONS

Kind words and checklists of ethical requirements exist in most organizations. What is needed is Fraud Smart ways of integrating expectations inside the business so that no one needs to review the code of ethics to work out what to do when deciding on a course of action – they *know* what is right and what is expected of them. This approach only works where the people at the top and those who get quickly promoted lead by example, rather than suggest to their staff 'do as I say not what I do!'

There are three main conclusions that we can draw from our discussions and suggestions in this chapter. These conclusions will be used to drive your Fraud Smart toolkit, which you will be designing at the end of this part of the book:

10.1 The code of ethics should be a living document rather than something that staff merely read.
10.2 The expected standards of conduct should be implemented through awareness strategies, sanctions and ongoing assessments of effectiveness.
10.3 The aim is for cultural integration where all parts of the business are well positioned to embrace values that drive the way people work and the decisions they make.

Anti-fraud strategies start with promoting expectations of behaviour that reinforce fairness, honesty at all times and openness wherever commercially feasible.

11
Whistleblowing

As we have already said, this book is based around the Fraud Smart cycle, which covers five key aspects of helping non-specialists get to grips with fraud at work. This is repeated in Figure 11.1.

This chapter sits within the third part of the Fraud Smart cycle, Embracing Sound Ethics, and covers the appropriate way for relaying concerns at work to ensure that they are properly addressed.

WHAT CAN GO WRONG?

Whistleblowing means different things to different people. Some see it as snitching on friends, while others feel it has something to do with going to the press to expose a scandal, and perhaps even being paid for this action. There is another view that whistleblowing involves telling officials about people who may have infringed some minor rule that has little value at all. If we fail to establish a sensible whistleblowing procedure, employees may become immersed in a culture of wrongdoing without being able to extract themselves.

We can consider how problems can arise by looking at three brief illustrative case studies taken from the UK and the USA. The first occurred in the public sector.

Figure 11.1   The Fraud Smart cycle.

CASE STUDY

A whistleblower claimed that staff working for a local authority's parking monitoring team had been dodging personal parking fines by cancelling them on the council's internal computer system. The monitoring team deal with public appeals to parking tickets that have been issued. Eight staff were under investigation by the council human resources department. A local councillor suggested, 'It would be a disgrace if there has been abuse of the system at the same time as the council is treating motorists as a cash cow.' A further allegation is that the staff's emergency parking permits were also being abused. A council spokeswoman said:

> These allegations are so far exactly that: allegations that are not proven. The council places great importance on whistleblowing by staff as part of our determination to prevent and root out any malpractice. We are committed to a zero-tolerance approach against any wrongdoing and our employees are well aware of that. All allegations are investigated thoroughly.

A more forward-looking view of whistleblowing is that it consists of a culture of openness, where staff can speak to their managers in conjunction with a 'speak-up line' allowing any outstanding concerns to be directed to the person best placed to deal with them. Alert staff can be a great asset when they are able to spot inconsistencies and then inform the appropriate authorities, as the next two cases attest:

CASE STUDY

An electrician who repeatedly claimed payment for jobs he never even turned up to was sentenced to 120 hours' community service. He was supposed to have undertaken over £3000 of work for a local authority and was ordered to repay £1830 and to pay costs. The apprentice electrician worked for the facilities management team, which supplies a shared service facility for a number of local authorities. He was supposed to carry out safety testing on electrical appliances. Not only did he claim that he had done the work when he had never even attended the sites, but he also claimed and was paid for overtime. The scam was brought to light when a member of the facilities management team noticed items of electrical equipment that had not been safety tested.

CASE STUDY

The deputy security manager at a large hospital was sentenced to six months' imprisonment for stealing from the parking ticket machines. The manager pleaded guilty to the theft of £16 360 after an investigation by a fraud team, who had been alerted by security staff who had seen him pocketing money from the hospital's parking machines on at least 35 occasions. He then tried to cover his tracks by collecting the money on days when he had booked annual leave and told other security staff that the machines were malfunctioning. When concerns were raised, the fraud team's investigation resulted in an arrest.

WHAT DO THE EXPERTS SAY?

The importance of encouraging fraud reporting is duly noted in our key texts:

> Fraud reporting mechanisms are a critical component of an effective fraud prevention and detection system. Organizations should implement

hotlines to receive tips from both internal and external sources. Such reporting mechanisms should allow anonymity and confidentiality, and employees should be encouraged to report suspicious activity without fear of reprisal. (ACFE Report, page 5)

The report goes on to explain how tip-offs are the foundation of fraud detection:

One of the principal goals of our research is to identify how past frauds were detected so that organizations can apply that knowledge to their future anti-fraud efforts. Tips were by far the most common detection method in our study, catching nearly three times as many frauds as any other form of detection. This is consistent with the findings in our prior reports. Tips have been far and away the most common means of detection in every study since 2002, when we began tracking the data. (ACFE Report, page 16)

It provides a fascinating breakdown of the sources of tips-offs that shows the wide range of potential informants that are available to most organizations:

In 67% of the cases where there was an anonymous tip, that tip was reported through an organization's fraud hotline. This strongly suggests that hotlines are an effective way to encourage tips from employees who might otherwise not report misconduct. Perhaps most important, organizations that had fraud hotlines suffered much smaller fraud losses than organizations without hotlines. Those organizations also tended to detect frauds seven months earlier than their counterparts.

Sources of tips:

Employee	*49.2%*
Customer	*17.8%*
Anonymous	*13.4%*
Vendor	*12.1%*
Shareholder/Owner	*3.7%*
Competitor	*2.5%*
Perpetrator's Acquaintance	*1.8% (ACFE Report, page 17)*

We turn now to the guidance from *Managing the Business Risk of Fraud* on the way reporting lines can be employed to best effect:

Marketing the existence of a hotline to increase awareness, making it easy to use, and promoting the timely handling of all reported issues are strong preventive measures that should supplement the detective control of hotlines. The hotline should be promoted with educational materials provided to shareholders, employees, customers, and vendors, all of whom can provide valuable information from a variety of reliable sources. Hotlines ideally support a multilingual capability and provide access to a trained interviewer 24 hours a day, 365 days a year. (MBRF, page 35)

Our final quote makes it clear that anonymity is an important consideration:

Provision for anonymity to any individual who willingly comes forward to report a suspicion of fraud is a key to encouraging such reporting and should be a component of the organization's policy. The most effective whistleblower hotlines preserve the confidentiality of callers and provide assurance to employees that they will not be retaliated against for reporting their suspicions of wrongdoing including wrongdoing by their superiors. Another key is demonstrating that their reporting will result in appropriate and timely action being taken. To preserve the integrity of the whistleblower process, it must also provide a means of reporting suspected fraud that involves senior management, possibly reporting directly to the audit committee. (MBRF, page 35)

OUR MODEL EXPLAINED

The experts recognize the role of fraud reporting lines, because so much fraud is discovered by tip-offs from a wide variety of different sources. When something untoward is happening, it is surprising how often other people know about it. In fact, some fraudsters take pride in boasting about their adventures to people they think will not inform on them.

We have developed a simple model in Figure 11.2 to illustrate one way of dealing with the issues raised in this chapter.

Our model suggests four main measures for instilling awareness and trust in a reporting system that encourages people to speak up about concerns at work. We can explore these issues by considering each separate part of our model in turn.

Figure 11.2   Whistleblowing factors.

Stance

Each organization should develop a clear stance on whistleblowing. Note that:

- It is a good idea to provide a policy, either as part of the main anti-fraud policy or as a separate but linked appendix.
- It is also good practice to work out what is covered by the whistleblowing policy and whether it includes information on all wrongdoing, such as safety breaches, favouritism and so on, as well as that relating to fraud and corruption.
- The whistleblowing procedure should be properly distinguished from the separate grievance procedure, under which staff may raise any major concerns about personal problems they may be experiencing, such as bullying by their line manager.

One way forward is to have a defined policy and make it a duty for people to report wrongdoing in line with this policy. It can also be made clear that any abuse of the policy may become a disciplinary offence. Most developed countries have whistleblowing laws and regulations that call for the protection of whistleblowers from any retaliation, either implicit or explicit, and this should also be explained to staff.

Manager

The manager has a key role in making the whistleblowing hotline procedure work properly:

- Each manager should ensure that their staff know the procedure, understand how they can make use of the hotline and that it is a duty to do so in the appropriate circumstances.
- All whistleblowing policies should incorporate the line manager as the first point of call unless there is a reason otherwise. Such reasons can include:
  - The matter is too complex, involving many different parts of the business.
  - The manager is away or there is a vacancy at that level.
  - The manager may be implicated.
  - The matter has already been referred to the manager with no real resolution.
  - The whistleblowing procedure asks the employee to provide information to an authorized person.

Thus there are reasons not to involve the line manager, but in the general course of business it is hoped that most concerns will find their way to the line manager and be resolved immediately through the normal management channels. Most importantly, each manager should operate an 'open-door policy' wherever feasible to encourage team members to come forward and discuss their concerns and suspicions. The Fraud Smart employee has to tread carefully. Being Fraud Smart is great, as it means that we recognize that some people, some of the time, will be deceitful or at least feel forced into a corner. That does not mean, however, that the manager's office should become the scene of a series of clandestine meetings where team members take turns to accuse each other of being unfair or being a little odd or suspicious, with the manager acting as both judge and jury. Every manager needs to set an attitude that says: 'Yes, we must trust everyone, but please make sure that you can also validate everything of importance if asked.'

Facilities

We hope to encourage employees to be attentive and managers to be helpful in addressing fraud, but nonetheless there are occasions when a whistleblowing hotline may be the best way of ensuring that wrongdoing is addressed. If an organization is to take reporting seriously, it must set up solid arrangements that support this facility, which should include at a minimum the following elements:

- *A dedicated reporting line manned by professionals.* A fraud investigation may well start with a tip-off and this information must be handled properly by trained individuals. The information is often confusing and it does take a trained person to question the informant, pick up the main threads and place them in a logical order.
- *Convenient 24-hour service.* Many people do not want to talk to a hotline at work and may well feel like contacting someone during the evening or at the weekend from their private phone or email. Note that a basic message machine does not constitute a proactive professional reporting line.
- *Encouragement to provide further information.* The reporting procedure should allow an ongoing relationship to be established with the caller. Assurances can be given regarding confidentiality and that the informant can remain anonymous. At the same time, the informant should be told also to respect the confidentiality of the case. Further contact can be encouraged by providing a password so that the informant can come back with more information without giving their name.
- *Feedback.* The ongoing relationship should involve feedback so that the informant is given a rough idea of the action that is being taken as a result of their contact. This should be done without going into too much detail and taking care not to give the impression that the informant is now part of the investigating team.

Be careful what you wish for – if an organization wants its people to use a speak-up line, it must be prepared to invest in a professional facility and respond fully to the resulting information.

Experience

This criterion is about the experiences people have when reporting their concerns. Note the following:

- It does not matter how wonderful the facilities are for whistleblowing or how impressive the written statements and policies on the need to come forward with information, they are no good unless they work in practice.
- Many organizations acquire a reputation for dealing with tip-offs in a way that says they are not always welcome or that they will not be dealt with if they make management look bad.

If one employee or associate is given a hard time after reporting a concern, this experience will be conveyed across the organization and would-be whistleblowers may feel that they will suffer if they decide to act. Most conspiracy theories are based around this concept that the powers-that-be do not like their work problems exposed.

Awareness and Trust

If the organization has a clear stance on whistleblowing and its managers understand the importance of encouraging staff to talk to them, we are on the way to a good reporting system. Moreover, we have noted that there should be professional facilities in place. If staff's experience is that concerns at work are taken seriously and they are treated fairly, it is possible to use tip-offs to reduce fraud and deal quickly with any such problems:

- If we have all these things in place we will have a degree of awareness and trust in the whistleblowing procedure, which will be a strong part of our Fraud Smart strategy.
- If these things are not in place the opposite will be true and we may end up with a secretive workplace where abuse and scams go on for years undetected.
- One way to reinforce the trust we need is to ensure that top management are on board and that the audit committee receives regular reports of cases (with no names stated) so that its members can exercise their oversight role in making sure that all concerns are addressed.

It is important that the whistleblowing arrangements are managed by a high-profile part of the organization such as legal, human resources, compliance or internal auditing. The party responsible for the hotline should appreciate one thing: most people will not willingly put themselves in the firing line unless there is a sensible support network that means doing so becomes much less scary than it would otherwise be.

OUR THREE KEY CONCLUSIONS

Tip-offs are key to fraud detection and also act as a deterrent. We have developed a whistleblowing model that is designed to encourage people to speak up about wrongdoing at work. This involves an infrastructure that costs time and money to put in place and operate, but it is an essential part of any Fraud Smart strategy. The fact is that many people view whistleblowing as an unattractive option that will tend to result in problems for the informant, either in their current job or when they seek work in the future. If the employer does not tackle this perception head on, it will be hard to implement a suitable and user-friendly facility to raise any concerns at work.

There are three main conclusions that we can draw from our discussions and suggestions in this chapter. These conclusions will be used to drive your Fraud Smart toolkit, which you will be designing at the end of this part of the book:

11.1 Every employer should set out a stance on whistleblowing that recognizes that people can be reluctant to speak up in the face of wrongdoing.
11.2 Suitable whistleblowing facilities should be in place that incorporate and do not undermine the role of the line manager.
11.3 All employees should possess an awareness of the whistleblowing facilities along with an understanding of how they can be used as a trusted device for discharging one's duty at work.

If we are to ensure that we operate an ethical organization that does not tolerate fraud, any cracks should be brought into the open and exposed through an effective whistleblowing facility.

12
Building Your Fraud Smart Toolkit

In this part of the book we have considered the way in which a moral compass can ensure the ethical behaviour of an organization with in-built facilities for employees and others to report any concerns about wrongdoing. We can restate that this book is based around the Fraud Smart cycle, which covers five key aspects of helping non-specialists get to grips with fraud at work. This is repeated in Figure 12.1.

This chapter sits within the third part of the Fraud Smart cycle, Embracing Sound Ethics, and covers the need to build an ethical basis to ensure that anti-fraud measures have a good chance of working to reduce fraud and abuse. Here we cover the task of helping you improve your personal Fraud Smart toolkit.

KEY LEARNING OBJECTIVES

Let's return to the learning objectives that were set for this part of the book:

Figure 12.1   The Fraud Smart cycle.

This chapter gives you the chance to reflect on the key conclusions that have been developed in the chapters in this part of the book and how they can become part of your personal development strategy.

Key Conclusions	Personal Fraud Smart Toolkit
9.1 The moral compass needs to be held steady to ensure that it balances the magnetic forces that may be in conflict and to avoid ending up off course.	Research the values that underpin your organization and reflect on the messages about personal conduct and overall direction that they provide. Do you feel that these values are adequately translated into working life? If you feel you need some guidance about the whole concept of business ethics, then talk to your manager.
9.2 The code of ethics should seek to reconcile the variables that underpin society's best interests and those of the organization in question.	Carefully consider where tensions could arise between the values set by your employer and the values that are promoted by stakeholder groups. Are there any areas where these tensions create blurred lines that may need to be clarified? If so, seek out advice from your manager on any such conflicts.

(Continued)

Key Conclusions	Personal Fraud Smart Toolkit
9.3 Each employee should be given guidance and leadership to ensure that they are able to fit their personal interests into the dimensions created by the corporate code of ethics.	Are there any ethical training programmes that you could book on to to gain a better insight into the way business ethics affect what happens at work, if you feel you would benefit from this intervention? If you have specific issues that mean your personal interests may at times conflict with your duties at work, you must talk to your manager about this matter.
10.1 The code of ethics should be a living document rather than something that staff merely read.	Talk to your boss or other members of the management team about the way ethics is driven into your organization. Is there any scope for improvement? Fraud Smart people will challenge any aspects of their work and their work area that mean business ethics could be undermined, as an official part of their duties at work.
10.2 The expected standards of conduct should be implemented through awareness strategies, sanctions and ongoing assessments of effectiveness.	Get hold of the staff disciplinary code of practice and review the way standards of conduct are addressed through appropriate sanctions where required. If you are in a position to set and review staff performance, is there any way of making ethical decisions a more integrated part of the way the performance of your staff is assessed?
10.3 The aim is for cultural integration where all parts of the business are well positioned to embrace values that drive the way people work and the decisions they make.	Undertake an exercise where you review the code of ethics and consider whether the messages can be read across to corporate strategies and business decisions made.

Key Conclusions	Personal Fraud Smart Toolkit
11.1 Every employer should set out a stance on whistleblowing that recognizes that people can be reluctant to speak up in the face of wrongdoing.	Talk to your colleagues about the culture in place regarding informing on illegal practices and whether this is something that is encouraged or not. Is there scope to develop a more positive environment? If you are a manager, remind your staff on a regular basis about the need to speak up about any concerns at work that fit with the whistleblowing procedure.
11.2 Suitable whistleblowing facilities should be in place that incorporate and do not undermine the role of the line manager.	Get hold of the corporate whistleblowing policy (or information on the speak-up line) and make sure that you are familiar with its contents and the process that is adopted. Reflect on whether you are someone whom people confide in and whether you ensure that there is time to talk to people in private so that they can discuss concerns they may have about wrongdoing at work. If you hardly ever meet with your managers, staff teams and opposite numbers in private, then this is unlikely to be the case. Try to be more open to people who need to trust you before confiding in you.
11.3 All employees should possess an awareness of the whistleblowing facilities along with an understanding of how they can be used as a trusted device for discharging one's duty at work.	Consider whether there are any concerns about questionable practices that you have come across during the course of your work that you should bring to the attention of your manager or an appropriate person, as defined in the whistleblowing policy. Also, think about issues that people have told you about and whether this information should be relayed to anyone else.

You can consider building your Fraud Smart toolkit and decide whether any of the above tasks should be incorporated into your personal development plan that is agreed with your boss.

Now have a go at the multichoice quiz for Part III of the book, check your answers against Appendix B and record your score in Appendix C.

PART III MULTICHOICE QUIZ

41 Insert the missing words.
The idea of employee security has faded over the years as the corporate model moves away from long-term employment at the same organization to much shorter time frames, which creates a great strain on . . . .
a shareholder value
b employee loyalty
c fraud suspects
d staff unions

42 Which is the least appropriate statement?
A process should be implemented for directors, employees and contractors to disclose potential or actual conflicts of interest within the organization. Once conflicts are internally disclosed, there are several decision paths:
a Management may assert that there is in fact a conflict and require the individual to terminate the activity or leave the organization.
b Management may accept the internal disclosure and determine that there is no conflict of interest in the situation described.
c Management may accept that no internal disclosure is required.
d Management may decide that there is a potential for conflict of interest and may impose certain constraints on the individual to manage the identified risk and to ensure that there is no opportunity for a conflict to arise.

43 Insert the missing words.
The concept of competing interests undermines the . . . .
. . . . , which sets a scope, width and breadth within which behaviour is deemed either acceptable or unacceptable, but this is put under strain when personal conflicts come into play.
a moral compass
b moral insights
c gifts register
d interpersonal skills

44 Which is the most appropriate statement?
a Our model suggests that people will tend to act in a way that satisfies their view on three key considerations: the employer's

best interests, the wider society's interests and their own team's
best interests.

b Our model suggests that people will tend to act in a way that
satisfies their view on three key considerations: the employee's
best interests, the wider society's interests and their personal best
interests.

c Our model suggests that people will tend to act in a way that
satisfies their view on three key considerations: the employer's
best interests, the local community's interests and their personal
best interests.

d Our model suggests that people will tend to act in a way that
satisfies their view on three key considerations: the employer's
best interests, the wider society's interests and their personal best
interests.

45 Insert the missing words.
Organizations that work towards society's best interests will
assume a good reputation, but it is often the case that, ironically,
. . . . business may be able to cut corners, be less
than totally ethical and provide cheaper products that sell well as a
result.

a a more sincere and less aggressive
b a less sincere and more aggressive
c a less sincere and less aggressive
d a more sincere and more aggressive

46 Which is the least appropriate statement?
Most organizations try to define their moral compass by setting out
a code of ethics for their business that covers areas such as:

a *Integrity* – where the workforce and associates are expected to
behave in an honest and fair way at all times.

b *Accountability* – where the entire workforce is expected to
stand up and be counted for their actions, including any
failure to act in safeguarding the business of which they are in
charge.

c *Openness* – where the executives disclose their marketing strategy
and their most sensitive risks on their website.

d *Transparency* – where the business is run in a way that is open
and clear, so that its activities can be appreciated by stakeholders
and are not shrouded in mystery.

47 Insert the missing word.
   In the past, it was enough simply to prepare a code of ethics, but
   nowadays it is more important to demonstrate that employees are
   living up to a set of standards that meet the expectations of
   . . . .
   a stakeholders
   b customers
   c managers
   d shareholders

48 Insert the missing word.
   It is one thing to prepare a code of ethics and statements about
   behaving fairly at work, but it is necessary to go further and
   implement these . . . . across the organization.
   a examples
   b rules
   c values
   d newsletters

49 Which is the most appropriate statement?
   a Regardless how many codes of ethics are in place within an
     organization, where a few staff members fail to abide by the
     values that underpin ethical behaviour there is no scope for anti-
     fraud policies to work.
   b Regardless how many codes of ethics are in place within an
     organization, where the top people fail to abide by the values that
     underpin top performance there is no scope for anti-fraud policies
     to work.
   c Regardless how many codes of ethics are in place within an
     organization, where the top people fail to abide by the values that
     underpin ethical behaviour there is no scope for accounting
     policies to work.
   d Regardless how many codes of ethics are in place within an
     organization, where the top people fail to abide by the values that
     underpin ethical behaviour there is no scope for anti-fraud
     policies to work.

50 Insert the missing words.
   The board of directors should ensure that its own . . . .
   . . . . . . set the tone for fraud risk management and that management

implements policies that encourage ethical behaviour, including processes for employees, customers, vendors and other third parties to report instances where those standards are not met.
a governance practices
b human resource policies
c procurement codes
d boardroom minutes

51 Which is the least appropriate statement?
Some organizations have developed corporate cultures that encompass strong corporate governance practices, including:
a Board ownership of agendas and information flow, access to multiple layers of management and effective control of a whistleblower hotline.
b Nominations and remuneration processes driven by the board.
c Effective senior management team (including chief executive officer, chief financial officer and chief operating officer) evaluations, performance management, compensation and succession planning.
d A code of conduct specific to senior management, in addition to the organization's code of conduct.

52 Insert the missing words.
The code of ethics sets standards about . . . .
and should address the usual areas such as integrity, accountability and transparency.
a superior behaviour
b dealing with customers
c dismissing staff
d expected behaviour

53 Which is the least appropriate statement?
The code of ethics sets standards about expected behaviour and should address the usual areas, such as integrity, accountability and transparency:
a It is about allowing the business to search for and create successful growth and also explore opportunities, but in a way that is fair and meets these expected standards of conduct.
b Since the code is for all employees, it should be set out in complex terms that capture the key messages the board wishes to deliver.

c At the same time, the code should be strong enough to deal with practical issues that face the type of business in question.

d The code should be designed so that it inspires the workforce to make the 'right' decisions even where there are some grey areas that are difficult to negotiate around.

54 Insert the missing words.

Posters, screensavers and regular mentions in staff communications can all be used to keep up the pressure on spreading awareness as a continuing process. For example, it is necessary to make clear on a regular basis how . . . . should be recorded in the relevant registers.

a staff breaks

b travel claims

c disciplinary breaches

d gifts and hospitality

55 Insert the missing words.

The final part of our model relates to . . . . That is, ethics should be embedded inside an organization so that the workforce behave well because they believe it is the right thing to do, rather than because they have been told to do so or risk getting sanctioned:

a cultural integration

b multicultural integration

c cultural segregation

d cultural awareness

56 Insert the missing word(s).

. . . . means different things to different people. Some see it as snitching on friends, while others feel that it has something to do with going to the press to expose a scandal, and perhaps even being paid for this action.

a bubble blowing

b finger pointing

c whistleblowing

d spying

57 Which is the most appropriate statement?

a Suspicious staff can be a great asset when they are able to spot inconsistencies and then inform the appropriate authorities.

b Alert staff can be a great asset when they are able to spot inconsistencies and then inform the appropriate authorities.

c Alert staff can be a great asset when they are able to spot bad apples and then inform the appropriate authorities.

d Alert staff can be a great asset when they are able to spot inconsistencies and then inform the newspapers.

58 Insert the missing words.

Organizations should implement hotlines to receive tip-offs from both internal and external sources. Such reporting mechanisms should allow . . . . , and employees should be encouraged to report suspicious activity without fear of reprisal.

a anonymity and secrecy

b anonymity and confidentiality

c confidentiality and gossip

d diplomatic immunity

59 Select the most appropriate breakdown of the sources of fraud tip-offs:

a Employee 1.8%, Customer 17.8%, Anonymous 13.4%, Vendor 12.1%, Shareholder/Owner 3.7%, Competitor 2.5%, Perpetrator's Acquaintance 49.2%.

b Employee 49.2%, Customer 3.7%, Anonymous 13.4%, Vendor 12.1%, Shareholder/Owner 17.8%, Competitor 2.5%, Perpetrator's Acquaintance 1.8%

c Employee 2.5%, Customer 17.8%, Anonymous 13.4%, Vendor 12.1%, Shareholder/Owner 3.7%, Competitor 49.2%, Perpetrator's Acquaintance 1.8%

d Employee 49.2%, Customer 17.8%, Anonymous 13.4%, Vendor 12.1%, Shareholder/Owner 3.7%, Competitor 2.5%, Perpetrator's Acquaintance 1.8%

60 Select the least appropriate statement:

Each organization should develop a clear stance on whistleblowing. Note that:

a It is an idea to provide a policy either as part of the main anti-fraud policy or as a separate but linked appendix.

b Make sure that employees are able to report on poor performance by colleagues.

c It is also an idea to work out what is covered by the whistleblowing policy and whether it covers all wrongdoing, such as safety breaches, favouritism and so on, as well as activities relating to fraud and corruption.

d The whistleblowing procedure should be properly distinguished from the separate grievance procedure, under which staff may raise any major concerns over personal problems that they may be experiencing, such as bullying by their line manager.

PART IV
Recognizing Red Flags

Learning Objective

To give you an outline of why fraud happens and how, by being alert, you can pick up red flags that may suggest fraud.

13
The Ingredients of Fraud

As you have already seen, this book is based around the Fraud Smart cycle, which covers five key aspects of helping non-specialists get to grips with fraud at work. This is repeated in Figure 13.1.

This chapter sits within the fourth part of the Fraud Smart cycle, Recognizing Red Flags, and covers the factors that tend to be in place when fraud occurs in the workplace. We are going to drill down in a little more detail into the concept of fraud and how it arises.

WHAT CAN GO WRONG?

There is a set of ingredients that can come together in a dangerous cocktail that promotes fraudulent behaviour. It is a good idea to appreciate these ingredients as a way of helping predict where fraud can happen, and then to look for red flags that suggest it is actually happening. Where the knowledge that fraud can lie hidden for some time is not present in managers and their staff teams, much could go wrong.

We can consider how problems can arise by looking at two brief illustrative case studies taken from the UK and the USA. The first describes a detailed fraud at a US law firm.

Figure 13.1   The Fraud Smart cycle.

CASE STUDY

A Dallas law firm sued a former employee to recoup the $100 000 she allegedly stole from it. One of the shareholders argued that these types of thefts are difficult for law firms to deal with due to the embarrassment they can cause. The former employee systematically altered cheques and entries in the firm's accounting records to conceal her embezzlement of between $100 000 and $200 000. She signed a plea agreement at the county district court that she would plead guilty and accept deferred community supervision for 10 years, along with a $2500 fine and restitution of $176 000.

She had been responsible for depositing collections; preparing cheques to pay the firm's creditors; maintaining accounting records; and reporting collections, payments and account balances to members of the firm's management committee. She reported revenues that were inconsistent with the prior year's revenues and operating net income, as expenses had dramatically increased to give a much reduced net income. The culprit informed the firm's management committee that she had made an accounting error and misstated gross revenues by approximately $300 000, which was used to allocate the partners' year-end income. Soon after that she failed to return to work or to transfer the cheques to the partners. The firm then commissioned an audit, which revealed the swindle. The employee was in a position of trust and thought that she would not be caught, as she controlled most of the day-to-day finances with very little segregation of duties.

Where funds move between accounts, there is always the chance that these funds can be diverted or wrongly authorized:

CASE STUDY

An employee in a local authority's finance department set up a bank account and was fraudulently moving funds from the authority into this account. Anomalies were noticed in the movement of funds and, following advice from the police, the authority called in a firm of investigators, who made a data image of the employee's computer. They found that the suspect was not only moving funds from the authority, but also from a number of other companies with which it had an association. The police were informed and the employee was suspended pending further investigation.

WHAT DO THE EXPERTS SAY?

The extracts from our key texts that are relevant to this chapter come from the ACFE Report. This details a threefold classification of employee fraud, with the first category being the most prevalent:

1 Asset misappropriations are those schemes in which the perpetrator steals or misuses an organization's resources. These frauds include schemes such as skimming cash receipts, falsifying expense reports and forging company checks.
2 Corruption schemes involve the employee's use of his or her influence in business transactions in a way that violates his or her duty to the employer for the purpose of obtaining a benefit for him- or herself or someone else. Examples of corruption schemes include bribery, extortion and a conflict of interest.
3 Financial statement fraud schemes are those involving the intentional misstatement or omission of material information in the organization's

financial reports. Common methods of fraudulent financial statement manipulation include recording fictitious revenues, concealing liabilities or expenses and artificially inflating reported assets. (ACFE Report, page 10)

These types of fraud can be maintained undetected for some time. It would appear that the more senior the fraudster, the longer they tend to continue before being found out:

As the following table illustrates, frauds committed by higher-level perpetrators also took longer to detect. Cases perpetrated by owners and executives typically lasted for two years before they were detected – nearly twice as long as employee frauds.

Months to Detection Based on Position

Position	Median Months to Detect
Employee	*13*
Manager	*18*
Owner/Executive	*24 (ACFE Report, page 49)*

OUR MODEL EXPLAINED

We have developed a simple model in Figure 13.2 to illustrate one way of dealing with the issues raised in this chapter.

Our model suggests that four factors need to come together for the threat of fraud to arise. More frightening is the view that fraud will definitely happen if these four factors coincide. We can explore the issues by considering each separate part of our model in turn.

Benefits

Fraud involves deceit to gain some sort of advantage; that is, there will be some benefit derived from commiting the fraud.

- In one case a young man secured a job with a local company by claiming to have a professional qualification, which turned out to be a misrepresention. One view is that people do exaggerate to get work and that this shows initiative. The opposing view is that this is an

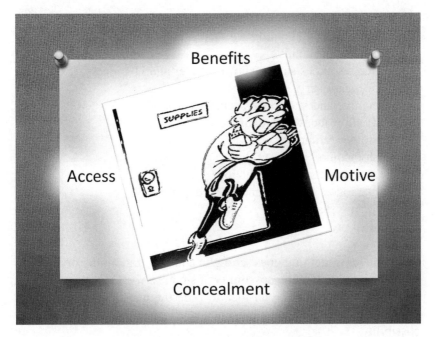

Figure 13.2 Ingredients of fraud.

outright attempt to gain a pecuniary advantage for personal gain – a well-paid job that he would otherwise not have got.

- We had a look at the areas ripe for fraud in Chapter 1, which suggested that income, expenditure, data and assets were all at risk as potential 'benefits' for prospective fraudsters.
- A disgruntled employee can bombard their ex-employer with viruses or can post malicious reviews; here the gain is subjective in terms of sheer revenge, rather than a clear financial gain, and causes criminal damage rather than fraud. If this same person asks for a pay-off or the attacks will continue, this is more like our common understanding of fraud.
- There will be many parts of a large organization that are at risk of being attacked and breached, including:
  - Payroll systems
  - Contracts
  - Expenditure
  - Purchasing
  - Income

- Expenses
- Equipment and IT hardware
- Computer programs
- Office resources such as power, water and IT processing capacity
- Office stationery
- Executive and staff bonus schemes
- Staff allowances and loans
- Customer refunds
- Cash income
- Bank accounts and transactions
- Office logos, ID cards and headed stationery
- Invoicing system
- And so on . . .

Whenever something goes wrong in an organization, the first course of action is to explore the possibility of simple error. Once this has been ruled out, then it may be an idea to pose the question: Who *benefits* from this activity? The response may well point to fraud as the next possibility.

Access

There are numerous assets and interests that have to be protected by any organization to prevent fraud and the next ingredient is access:

- Fraud can only happen when the fraudster is able to access the benefit or gain they are after. Most organizations understand this ingredient very well and so seek to protect their resources by numerous access controls.
- Where the fraud is perpetrated by an employee, preventing it becomes more difficult, as this person will know how access is achieved and may be able to circumvent controls to perform unauthorized transactions, such as transferring funds to a bank account that they have set up for the purpose.
- In one case a computer programmer was able to divert small rounding differences on foreign currency exchanges to an account under his control. The hundreds of thousands of currency transactions resulted in a large sum of money arriving to this account over the course of several years.
- The final point regarding access is that the fraudster may not necessarily be a senior member of staff, but will need the intellectual

capacity to sit down and plan an attack that breaches systems security settings.

Access is about having an opportunity to commit fraud. At times it is this opportunity that can spark a fraud, in that the person in question realizes they can divert funds without being detected. Or there may be a flaw in the system such that large numbers of small-value transactions can be misappropriated over a period of time that gives a substantial accumulated gain for the fraudster. The sad fact is that the higher someone's position and the more they are trusted, the more this person tends to be given unrestricted access to funds, assets and financial transactions, giving them more scope to commit fraud.

Motive

Even if there is some benefit to be gained from taking a deceitful course of action and the employee can access the system or transaction in question, fraud will not necessarily occur:

- The employee will need to be motivated to commit fraud for that fraud to happen. We discuss the concept of rationalization – having a good excuse for being dishonest – in the next chapter.
- Motivation can come from employees feeling that they have to resort to fraud as there are no other options left.
- Because motives for fraud often relate to financial burdens, some organizations have installed staff counselling facilities where employees can ask for help with financial management or even short-term loans where they experience difficulties that they simply cannot resolve.
- This counselling referral can extend to drugs, alcohol, gambling and stress support where employees operate in highly pressured environments. Other organizations undertake regular credit scoring checks to make sure that staff who have access to company funds are not having problems managing their financial affairs.

Motive means having a reason to do something and this means that there is intent to do it. Most fraud investigations have to show that there was an intent to defraud before a case can be brought before the criminal courts. On the whole, motive will be based around meeting some kind of unfulfilled need.

Concealment

If employees want to commit fraud and they have the means to do so, things start to get scary and problems may well arise. The next ingredient relates to concealment, or what we can call the art of not getting caught:

- Smash-and-grab frauds are straightforward. Someone enters a property or attacks a person, or hacks into a system and steals funds, equipment or company goods. The crime happens, the damage is cleaned up and then it is investigated.
- The threat of fraud carried out by an intelligent employee who knows the system inside out has a different and more dangerous edge to it. Many would-be fraudsters are deterred from breaking the rules by the fear of getting caught and the consequences, the worst of which is going to jail.
- An employee who can access funds and record the details of changes to those same funds can then commit fraud and conceal it. Moreover, sometimes fraud happens and money is lost, but it is impossible to determine how it happened or who took it.
- An employer cannot go around accusing its workforce and there are times when the amount that is stolen is written off and controls strengthened, but no one is actually convicted of an offence.
- Other frauds remain undetected because they are concealed so well.

The ability to conceal a fraud tends to be related to the way controls can be overriden or records falsified to make it seem that there are no discrepancies. The reality of business life is that assets will always equal liabilities, so that someone owns the net worth of a business along with its income less expenditure. Where there is a gap due to fraud this equation will not add up, unless the records are in some way fudged to conceal the fraudulent deed.

OUR THREE KEY CONCLUSIONS

In this chapter we have identified a worrying cocktail of specific ingredients that, if they come together, may well lead to fraud. Some commentators argue that employee frauds do not just happen, they are often allowed to happen because the warning signs were not heeded by carefully considering the reasons behind them.

There are three main conclusions that we can draw from our discussions and suggestions. These conclusions will be used to drive your Fraud Smart toolkit, which you will be designing at the end of this part of the book:

13.1 A good understanding of the types of areas that can create a gain to the prospective fraudster can be used to help minimize the threat of fraud.

13.2 Managers and staff groups should acknowledge the point where there is opportunity to defraud an employer and this coincides with a willingness to do so.

13.3 It is important that all staff activities are properly authorized, such that illegal activities are not able to be concealed and that they lead back to the culprit, to prevent fraud being perpetrated without fear of getting caught.

The knowledge of fraud throughout the organization need not be overly detailed, but it is helpful if everyone knows about the basic ingredients of fraud as described in this chapter, as a way of strengthening the anti-fraud strategies that are in place to help protect the organization.

14
Why People Slip Up

As we have said already, this book is based around the Fraud Smart cycle, which covers five key aspects of helping non-specialists get to grips with fraud at work. This is repeated in Figure 14.1.

This chapter sits within the fourth part of the Fraud Smart cycle, Recognizing Red Flags, and covers some of the reasons people get involved in fraudulent behaviour. This is a complex subject: many universities run three-year degrees in criminology that examine the reasons behind misbehaviour from people who appear to be sensible and trustworthy. In this chapter we only take a very brief look at the world of the fraudster.

WHAT CAN GO WRONG?

Most organizations maintain a positive culture where their worforce is given loads of responsibilities and is empowered to make decisions at a local level wherever possible. However, the reality of corporate life is that some people, some of the time, can slip up. Where these same people have authority over corporate resources or simply have access rights and we fail to recognize this sad fact, much could go wrong.

We can consider how problems can arise by looking at three brief illustrative case studies taken from the UK and the USA, the first involving a hapless fraudster who blamed his 'dominating wife' for his bad behaviour:

Figure 14.1 The Fraud Smart cycle.

CASE STUDY

A husband stole £205 000 to fund his shopaholic wife's spending sprees. The senior bank loans adviser used his inside knowledge to fake loans in the name of friends and family. But he was spared jail after the judge was told he had been the timid victim of a domineering wife, who bought a vast amount of clothes she never wore, fast cars and holidays. The deception came to light when the bank contacted his mother-in-law to warn her that her loan payments were in arrears, while she was not even aware of the loan.

Other cases indicate that where there is opportunity there can be abuse, often by people who should really know better:

CASE STUDY

A former auditor with the state Department of Revenue was charged in federal court with creating false tax refunds and using the proceeds for personal benefit. She was charged with one count of conspiracy to commit mail fraud and one count of money laundering, along with her sister and niece. As an auditor her job was to process tax overpayments and she falsified records to create the impression that a taxpayer was owed a refund due to an overpayment when, in fact, that was not the case. Then, she prepared a refund cheque or a transfer of funds made payable to her sister or niece for the false refund amount. To make it more difficult for anyone to detect that the refunds were not legitimate, she used variations of her co-conspirators' names on the cheques and transfers. To cash the cheques, her co-conspirators sometimes allegedly sought the services of a cheque-cashing business and then divided the proceeds. On other occasions, the cheques were allegedly deposited into an account, in an effort to conceal the source of the funds, and then withdrawn and shared by the co-conspirators. In all, the three individuals were responsible for more than 200 fraudulent tax refund payments, totalling approximately $1.9 million.

A lifestyle imbalance where income does not add up to someone's required expenditure can be a major motivator for a potential fraudster:

CASE STUDY

A former longstanding finance executive of a medium-sized company pleaded guilty to 10 felony charges and received a sentence of 18 years in prison for the embezzlement of $9.9 million from her employer. The defendant had previously been arrested 13 times on drug and prostitution charges and she blamed addictions to gambling and prescription drugs for her fraud. However, the sentencing judge strongly rejected that explanation, chastised the defendant and stated his belief that the primary motivators were a selfish love of pleasure and pretty things, including regular shopping trips to New York and Europe to purchase 160 designer purses, 400 pairs of designer shoes and four guitars worth $100 000. Investigators had also said that the defendant used the stolen money to finance a gambling habit that saw her win and lose as much as $42 million in local casinos over seven years.

WHAT DO THE EXPERTS SAY?

Our two key texts contain extremely useful guidance on what makes a fraudster tick. The first quote shows how someone can go bad out of the blue:

> More than 85% of fraudsters in our study had never been previously charged or convicted for a fraud-related offense. This finding is consistent with our prior studies. (ACFE Report, page 5)

The report goes on to demonstrate how those at the top can cause the most damage:

> We asked survey respondents whether the perpetrator was an employee, a manager or an owner/executive. Below we see that the distribution of cases based on the perpetrator's position was fairly similar to what we found in our 2008 study, although the 2010 distribution was slightly more skewed toward employees and managers. Not surprisingly, there was a strong correlation between the perpetrator's position of authority and the losses caused by fraud. The median loss in owner/executive frauds was more than three times the loss caused by managers, and more than nine times higher than losses in employee fraud cases. (ACFE Report, page 48)

If fraud investigators could predict which employees would commit fraud, then there probably would not be any internal fraud. The truth is that there is no real way of knowing who will succumb. There is help at hand, however, and the ACFE Report offers some much-needed guidance:

- *Perpetrator's Gender.* Two-thirds of the frauds in our study were committed by males, which is a higher percentage than we encountered in 2008, but consistent with the overall trend noted in prior reports that most occupational frauds are committed by men. (page 52).
- *Perpetrator's Age.* Our past reports have generally shown the highest levels of fraud to occur in the 36–50 age range, but this year we found more than half of all cases were committed by individuals between the ages of 31 and 45. (page 56)
- *Perpetrator's Tenure.* More than 40% of perpetrators had between one and five years of experience at the victim organization when they committed the fraud, while a very small percentage had been with the victim organization for less than a year. About half of all fraudsters had been with the victim for more than five years. (page 57)

- *Perpetrator's Department.* 80% of all frauds in this study were committed by employees in six departments: accounting, operations, sales, executive/upper management, customer service and purchasing. (page 60)

OUR MODEL EXPLAINED

Fraudsters come in all shapes and sizes. The most trusted person may find themselves in a situation where they have unfettered access to company resources and may find they could remove funds and conceal this action by fiddling with the system that they know so well. So why do a small group of employees do so while the vast majority would not dream of it? There is no clear answer, but we have developed a simple model in Figure 14.2 to illustrate one way of dealing with the issues raised in this chapter.

Our model suggests that it is possible to devise a simple process through which we can predict whether someone who has always been honest will slip into fraudulent behaviour. Criminal gangs and career fraudsters stand out on their own, as they are crooked as a career choice

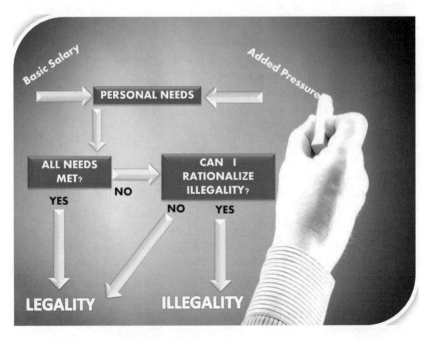

Figure 14.2 Legitimizing fraud.

and need no explanation above sheer greed. Managers who are blackmailed or have their family members kidnapped (so-called tiger kidnaps) using threats and menace may have little option than to assist a criminal, which is perfectly understandable.

Regarding people who simply slip into fraud, we can explore several issues by considering each separate part of our model in turn.

Basic Salary Versus Added Pressure

Many people see motivation in their work environment in terms of whether they are satisfied with their terms and conditions. They consider their basic salary and any benefits and work out whether they need to remain with the company, seek promotion or perhaps look for work elsewhere. This is a straightforward equation and most people accept that if they are not happy they can take legal measures to address the matter.

One view is that if extra pressure is applied to the question of whether a basic salary will suffice, the equation can change. This added pressure can comprise a wide variety of factors, such as:

- Gambling, drugs, alcohol or other addictions that cause financial stress.
- Pressure from peer groups to adopt a lavish lifestyle that involves spending or investing large amounts of money.
- Financial pressures due to health problems, impoverished friends and relatives and accumulated personal debt.
- Sheer greed where there is an irrational craving for expensive goods, which may stem from a spouse or close friend.

Personal Needs Met?

The next stage of our model asks whether the basic salary combined with added pressure meets the personal needs of the employee in question:

- If someone has a gambling problem but is able to work overtime and use credit facilities to fund their gambling, then their personal needs will be met.
- If someone has a spouse who wants expensive holidays and the employee can talk about the problem and perhaps get help in balancing domestic budgets, then this problem may be tackled.

- If, on the other hand, the added financial pressures cannot be met, then the employee may start to think about other options.
- It is at this stage that the idea of fraud may come to mind as a one-off idea or a carefully planned method to breach a system and mis-appropriate funds.

Rationalization

Rationalization is an interesting concept that has been used by criminologists for some time. We can view it as the ability to convince oneself that something that most people deem dishonest can be justified because there is a pressing need to take urgent action over and above the desire to remain honest. That is, the dishonest act is rationalized so that it can be carried out without intense guilt and a desire to confess.

Frauds are easier to rationalize when there is a ready-made excuse that someone can tell themselves and others if the need arises, such as:

- The company does not care about me, so I don't care about it.
- Everyone is up to no good, so why not me?
- I really need these funds and there is just no other choice.
- No one is going to miss this relatively small amount.
- As soon as things pick up, I will pay it all back.
- I work so hard and never get paid what I'm worth, so I'll even things up.
- If they cannot be bothered to protect their resources, what do they expect?
- If anyone asks I'll just say that it was an error and whatever happens I will not go to jail, which is the main thing.
- The top people get so much and I get so little – that's unfair.
- It's all a bit of an exciting joke. In fact, it makes work a bit less boring.
- I just want to show how clever I am.
- Look who's got the power now!

Legality Versus Illegality

The bottom line is that notwithstanding any personal needs, nothing illegal will happen 99 per cent of the time and all is well. However, if the right set of circumstances comes together at the right time, illegality will be the most probable result.

OUR THREE KEY CONCLUSIONS

Most times when an employee-based fraud occurs, a gasp of surprise can be heard as the office gossips express their shock at why manager X or team member Y has committed such a terrible act. In fact, there are many reasons for employees succumbing and we can plot someone's downfall by references to the basic factors that can lead to illegality.

There are three main conclusions that we can draw from our discussions and suggestions in this chapter. These conclusions will be used to drive your Fraud Smart toolkit, which you will be designing at the end of this part of the book:

14.1 Managers need to concede that fraudsters do not come from families of crooks and thieves, but often are trusted and well-liked professionals who have simply slipped into dishonesty.

14.2 It should be fully recognized that where someone's personal need provides a greater force than the need to remain honest, fraud can arise.

14.3 Anti-fraud policies need to reflect the fact that fraud can be rationalized to appear a just course of action by an otherwise honest person.

The risk of fraud is all the greater since many fraudsters have no previous convictions, hold responsible jobs and their activities can be very hard to detect.

15
Recognizing Red Flags

As you have seen, this book is based around a Fraud Smart cycle that covers five key aspects of helping non-specialists get to grips with fraud at work. This is repeated in Figure 15.1.

This chapter sits within the fourth part of the Fraud Smart cycle, Recognizing Red Flags, and covers some of the actual red flags that may indicate that a fraud is happening or is likely to happen. If those in the workforce are tuned in to these red flags, they will be able to alert the right people to any suspicions they might have.

WHAT CAN GO WRONG?

If the workforce is Fraud Smart, there is a much better chance of deterring would-be fraudsters and catching those who have a go at defrauding their employer. If we fail to achieve this basic goal, much could go wrong.

We can consider how problems can arise by looking at several brief illustrative case studies taken from the UK and the USA, starting with a work experience student:

CASE STUDY

A schoolgirl who stole thousands of pounds while on work experience with a top international law firm was jailed for five months. Within three days of joining the firm she used the computer system to generate company cheques. She forged her boss's signature and paid them into her bank account. She claimed to a probation officer that her boyfriend forced her to betray her boss, took the money she obtained and then disappeared with every penny. She had been assigned to the law firm for a couple of weeks when she was 15 and approached the same firm to do her work experience three years later. The judge said that the fact that her crimes started 72 hours after she returned to the firm made it seem to him that she went back with that in mind.

Figure 15.1   The Fraud Smart cycle.

Some fraudsters involve their family or contacts and often do not tell them what is going on:

CASE STUDY

A former Internal Revenue Service employee from Valencia, New Mexico has been ordered to pay $127 116 after pleading guilty to filing false tax returns for himself and members of his family. His returns failed to report all relevant income and included excessive deductions. His relatives were unaware that the tax returns he filed for them were fraudulent; moreover, he was able to steal over $10 000 in tax refunds from his relatives from these returns. He falsely claimed $16 819 in mortgage interest for a home that was given to him by his mother and a $12 000 deduction for 'alimony paid'. As US Department of Treasury agents searched his home after informing him he was being investigated for filing false tax returns, he screamed, 'I'm going to kill all of you!' The agents found three loaded guns, including a pair of .357 calibre revolvers and a .25 calibre semi-automatic pistol and about 115 rounds of ammunition. In exchange for his guilty plea, prosecutors agreed to dismiss a charge of threatening federal officers.

Other fraudsters make simple mistakes that mean they are eventually found out:

CASE STUDY

A crooked bank worker who helped a gang steal £65 000 from customers' accounts fainted when she was jailed for 12 months. The customer services worker passed on confidential details to fraudsters, who were then able to cash bogus cheques and make withdrawals. She was caught out because she repeatedly typed in her username and password to search for data at the branch. She admitted hacking into eight accounts, but claimed that an ex-boyfriend forced her to hand over information or members of her family would come to harm.

One red flag is transactions that do not fit with what is known about the person in question:

CASE STUDY

One defendant wrote 582 cheques amounting to $7.6 million on her employer's bank account to cover personal credit card payments and cash advances, and used a company cheque card to cover approximately $1.5 million in personal expenses. Investigators reported that the defendant hid her theft by forging accounting spreadsheets and destroying bank records. They also said that bank records only dated back two years, so that was as far back as the investigation went; it is unknown whether any thefts occurred prior to this time. Unfortunately, it took an outsider coming forth with valuable information to bring down this devastating six-year scheme. A bank's credit card investigator notified the company's president that the defendant was making weekly payments of about $25 700 to her personal credit card balance using company cheques.

WHAT DO THE EXPERTS SAY?

The ACFE Report makes it quite clear that their studies reinforce the importance of tips as a great source of information on fraudulent activities:

> *Occupational frauds are much more likely to be detected by tip than by any other means. This finding has been consistent since 2002 when we began tracking data on fraud detection methods. (ACFE Report, page 4)*

These tip-offs are great, but it does not mean that an organization's management team can sit back and rely on information received for detecting all frauds. They must do so much more. Senior management and, more importantly, the board member who oversees the anti-fraud strategy will have a whole array of tools in use to check for fraud and 'cleanse' the business of suspect transactions and suspicious behaviour:

> *Management review and internal audit were the second and third most common forms of detection, uncovering 15% and 14% of frauds, respectively. It is also noteworthy that 11% of frauds were detected through channels that lie completely outside of the traditional anti-fraud control structure: accident, police notification and confession. In other words, 11% of the time, the victim organization either had to stumble onto the fraud or be notified of it by a third party in order to detect it. (ACFE Report, page 16)*

But what about the actual workforce? Managers and front-line people may have no specialist knowledge of fraud, but should they be alert to red flags? This question is also addressed by our experts:

> *Fraudsters exhibit behavioral warning signs of their misdeeds. These red flags – such as living beyond one's means or exhibiting control issues – will not be identified by traditional controls. Auditors and employees alike should be trained to recognize the common behavioral signs that a fraud is occurring and encouraged not to ignore such red flags, as they might be the key to detecting or deterring a fraud. (ACFE Report, page 5)*

OUR MODEL EXPLAINED

We have developed a simple model in Figure 15.2 to illustrate one way of dealing with the issues raised in this chapter.

Our model suggests that there are at least three sets of criteria that can be used by everyone who works for or is associated with an organization to make Fraud Smart assumptions about possible

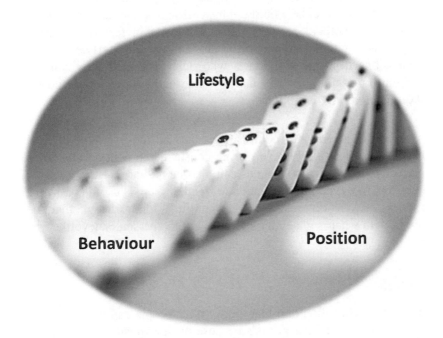

Figure 15.2   Categories of red flags.

dishonesty at work. We can explore these issues by considering each separate part of our model in turn.

Lifestyle

Some things in life are pretty obvious. If someone is living above their means, there could be a number of quite reasonable explanations:

• Their additional income could come from a spouse, another family member, a lucky break at the races, a deceased relative or perhaps a business interest and wise investments. But if none of these explanations applies, the question is where the extra money came from. In hindsight, there are many instances where an employee has been ripping off their employer and flaunting their newly acquired wealth.

• In one case an accounts clerk who worked for the London Metropolitan Police (New Scotland Yard) stole funds from a special account set up to pay informants. This account was not subject to a great deal of scrutiny since the information was highly sensitive and the accounts clerk could explain movement on the accounts with a well-rehearsed story. Meanwhile, he would tell his colleagues that he was off to his castle in Scotland for the weekend; he did in fact own a castle purchased with the stolen money. This extravagant lifestyle raised no questions from his workmates who only expressed their concerns about how this individual had so much money after the fraud was discovered.

Having lots of money could suggest that an illegal source of funds has been exploited. However, being constantly in debt and having to borrow money from colleagues can also be a sign that the person in question may eventually succumb to fraud, if there is no other way out. Lifestyle signals do have to be read carefully, but a lifestyle that does not fit with what is generally known about the person is nevertheless a red flag.

Position

Research makes the point that more senior people can do much more damage and for longer periods because of their position at work. We can also note the following:

- A tried-and-trusted senior manager will tend to have a great deal of authority to approve transactions and alter records simply because of their special position, which means that they have access to company resources that most others do not have.
- Where the fraud is high-level financial misstatement through inflating earnings, misreporting expenditure or hiding capital financing from the balance sheet to show misleading results, this can only be done by a few powerful executives. In this instance red flags relate to factors about the company, its environment and whether it operates in volatile markets with high earning expectations and linked bonus schemes, or executives who have given personal guarantees on company debt.
- Managers in positions where they can override controls pose a serious threat. Where such overrides occur in sensitive areas, it is important that someone, somewhere, such as a non-executive director, will be able to challenge these decisions. Remember, sensitive positions are not assigned only to senior people.
- If there is someone in the organization who has always been responsible for an entire set of transactions, they may be able to access a system or a resource with no questions asked, for example if they are employed in the following roles:
  - Accounts clerk
  - Payroll operator
  - Purchasing officer
  - Local agent for overseas contacts
  - Member of an in-house contracts-negotiating team
  - Personal investment adviser
  - Information security officer

To the first criterion of a lavish lifestyle we can add our second criterion of holding a special position with access to resources, systems and spending decisions. We now have two of the main red flags that may mean that a fraud could occur.

Behaviour

Our final category is behaviour. When someone behaves in an unusual manner, this could be for many different reasons, for example they might simply be awkward and that is that. Or it could be that their behaviour is designed to distract or even stop anyone from examining their activities and finding out that something is wrong.

Red flag behaviours can cover a wide range of attributes, a small sample of which is included in this list:

• *Being overly aggressive.* It is surprising how people will back off and avoid someone who is known to be aggressive or simply unhelpful. An aggressive fraudster will seek to intimidate colleagues and even managers to discourage them from asking questions or reviewing actions that fall outside standard controls. An employee who holds the threat of legal redress over their employer may simply feel victimized or may have a cunning plan to avoid probes into their work activities.

• *Being overly friendly.* On the other hand, some very good fraudsters take an opposing view and are extremely helpful. They offer to perform some of the checks that their manager should do, and so avert supervisory controls being applied. Friendly fraudsters also exploit the adage that 'nice people just do not do nasty things'. In this way the fraudster seeks close personal relationships with their supervisor to encourage the person who should be managing them to banish the thought that their staff member could ever engage in dishonesty.

• *Using distracting devices.* A fraudster may create an abundance of false alarms to keep their manager busy and distracted from what is really happening at work. This can range from inducing emergencies on a regular basis through to maintaining their files in such a poor state that it is impossible to check their activities.

• *Being excessively protective over their work area.* If a staff member starts work early, works late and does not want any cover when they have to take time off, this may be to ensure that no one gets involved in their work area. One technique is for the fraudster to set up their own sub-systems and special databases on the pretext that it helps them get their job done, when the real reason is that it means no one else can operate the system and perhaps discover the discrepancies.

• *Adopting close relationships with key players.* A fraudster may realize that they can work with another person to abuse a system and they may get very close to a customer, supplier or colleague to plan their fraud. For instance, a payroll officer and a human resources person could get together and set up false accounts on the company payroll system generating monthly payments that appear to be valid.

The behaviour of the suspect is one thing in terms of giving clues that there are problems. But it is also the behaviour of the business activity that can add to our stock of indications of fraud. Red flags can also include missing files, altered records, odd journal transfers, photocopies in files, unusual patterns of transactions and a whole assortment of oddities.

OUR THREE KEY CONCLUSIONS

We will look at detective controls in Part V of the book, which is about using proactive techniques to look for fraud at work. In this chapter we have examined the way in which Fraud Smart employees can be alert to signs that all is not well. Two or more red flags may come together to suggest that something needs to be probed further. A Fraud Smart workforce should be fully armed with a decent knowledge of these red flags.

There are three main conclusions that we can draw from our discussions and suggestions in this chapter. These conclusions will be used to drive your Fraud Smart toolkit, which you will be designing at the end of this part of the book:

15.1 While it is good to trust managers, colleagues and associates at work, it is also important that the entire workforce appreciates the need to be alert to signs that suggest otherwise.
15.2 Everyone should have a good knowledge of the way a person's lifestyle and position at work can be used as warning flags that something may be wrong or inappropriate and may suggest the possibility of fraud at work.
15.3 Everyone should be alert to unusual behaviour at work that may suggest that the person in question is engaged in fraud.

Along with appreciating what fraud is and its ramifications, it is important that if suspicious circumstances come to a person's attention, they are prepared to bring their concerns to the appropriate authorities.

16
Building Your Fraud Smart Toolkit

In this part of the book we have considered the way in which indicators of fraud or what are known as red flags can be used to equip the workforce with a valuable tool against fraud. As you are aware, this book is based around the Fraud Smart cycle, which covers five key aspects of helping non-specialists get to grips with fraud at work. This is repeated in Figure 16.1.

This chapter sits within the fourth part of the Fraud Smart cycle, Recognizing Red Flags, and covers the task of helping you improve your personal Fraud Smart toolkit.

KEY LEARNING OBJECTIVES

Let's return to the learning objectives that were set for this part of the book:

To give you an outline of why fraud happens and how, by being alert, you can pick up red flags that may suggest fraud.

OUR FRAUD CYCLE

Mastering Suitable Controls

Understanding the Threat

Recognizing Red Flags

Appreciating Respective Roles

Embracing Sound Ethics

Figure 16.1   The Fraud Smart cycle.

This chapter gives you the chance to reflect on the key conclusions that have been developed in the chapters in this part of the book and how they can become part of your personal development strategy.

Key Conclusions	Personal Fraud Smart Toolkit
13.1 A good understanding of the types of areas that can create a gain to the prospective fraudster can be used to help minimize the threat of fraud.	Have a think about aspects of your work area that could be open to abuse by an employee or outside party. Do you work in an area that could be said to have a high risk of fraud?
13.2 Managers and staff groups should acknowledge the point where there is opportunity to defraud an employer and this coincides with a willingness to do so.	Using the knowledge from 13.1, consider whether there are any gaps in the system that mean fraud could be committed by a knowledgeable person.

(Continued)

Key Conclusions	Personal Fraud Smart Toolkit
13.3 It is important that all staff activities are properly authorized, such that illegal activities are not able to be concealed and that they lead back to the culprit, to prevent fraud being perpetrated without fear of getting caught.	Consider whether there are any aspects of your business where a lack of proper authorization could mean a fraud could be committed. Fraud Smart people think about fraud risks and make sure that they are properly addressed.
14.1 Managers need to concede that fraudsters do not come from families of crooks and thieves, but often are trusted and well-liked professionals who have simply slipped into dishonesty.	Is there anyone in your organization who has such a wide range of authorizations and access that they could commit fraud, even if they are a tried-and-trusted, long-standing employee? Are there any indicators that this person could be committing fraud?
14.2 It should be fully recognized that where someone's personal need provides a greater force than the need to remain honest, fraud can arise.	Are you aware of anyone in your organization who appears to be under pressure to such an extent that they may succumb to fraud? Are there any indicators that this person could be committing fraud? Have another look at the chapter on red flags and see if anyone fits two or more of the criteria as part of this assessment.

Key Conclusions	Personal Fraud Smart Toolkit
14.3 Anti-fraud policies need to reflect the fact that fraud can be rationalized to appear a just course of action by an otherwise honest person.	Do some research into why people commit fraud against their employer as an extension to the basic material that we have provided in this book. Reflect on each of the examples of 'rationalization' that we use in the book and try to see employee fraud as something that can lie dormant in an otherwise honest person. Do a search for what is called the 'Fraud Triangle', developed by Dr Donald Cressey in the 1970s, for more insights into why people commit fraud.
15.1 While it is good to trust managers, colleagues and associates at work, it is also important that the entire workforce appreciates the need to be alert to signs that suggest otherwise.	Have an open discussion with your boss or another member of the management team and ask this person how you can reconcile the need to trust your colleagues and the need to be alert to the possibility of fraud committed by workmates. Each person will have their own version of trusting people, but making sure that things are still done properly. Also, if you make sure that all transactions are verified, this act also protects the person being examined, as it means they can prove that their actions were appropriate if doubt is raised at a later time.
15.2 Everyone should have a good knowledge of the way a person's lifestyle and position at work can be used as warning flags that something may be wrong or inappropriate and may suggest the possibility of fraud at work.	Make sure that you are completely comfortable with what we have called red flags, which may indicate that fraud is happening. Is there anything else you can add to our list?

(Continued)

Key Conclusions	Personal Fraud Smart Toolkit
15.3 Everyone should be alert to unusual behaviour at work that may suggest that the person in question is engaged in fraud.	Be aware of the signs that someone is lying to you and explore instances where this appears to be the case and involves areas at risk of fraud. A simple lie may be a colleague saying that an invoice has been checked when it is clear that there is a mistake and a third party was overpaid. Deceitful behaviour may include body language such as the following: • Nervous behaviour such as blinking and fidgeting due to stress. • Vague and inconsistent answers to simple questions. • Extremely precise and planned answers to simple questions. • Covering the mouth or nose to 'take back' the words. • Avoidance behaviour and odd excuses for a lack of cooperation. • Distracting behaviour, trying to change the topic. Some commentators argue that one needs to know the person well and their normal state before being able to judge when this person is behaving strangely. Note that professional liars will be able to act in a convincing way that makes it hard to detect any deceit. Are there any other indicators that someone in your organization could be committing fraud? Also, do you feel that there is someone at work who is becoming increasingly isolated that you might care to talk to, in case they are tempted to slip up or are already breaking the rules? Why don't you go and talk to them rather than feeling it is nothing to do with you?

You can consider building your Fraud Smart toolkit and decide whether any of the above tasks should be incorporated into your personal development plan that is agreed with your boss.

Now have a go at the multichoice quiz for Part IV of the book, check your answers against Appendix B and record your score in Appendix C.

PART IV MULTICHOICE QUIZ

61 Which is the most appropriate statement?
   a Asset misappropriations are those schemes in which the perpetrator steals or misuses an organization's income.
   b Asset abuses are those schemes in which the perpetrator steals or misuses an organization's resources.
   c Asset misappropriations are those schemes in which the perpetrator steals or misuses an organization's resources.
   d Asset misappropriations are those schemes in which the perpetrator steals or wastes an organization's resources.

62 Insert the missing words.
   Frauds committed by . . . . perpetrators take longer to detect.
   a lower-level
   b higher-level
   c middle-level
   d serious-minded

63 Insert the missing word.
   Fraud involves . . . . to gain some sort of advantage; that is, there will be some benefit derived from committing the fraud.
   a deceit
   b threats
   c loopholes
   d knowledge

64 Which is the most appropriate statement?
   a Whenever something goes wrong in an organization, the first course of action is to explore the possibility of fraud. Once this

has been ruled out, then it may be an idea to pose the question: Who benefits from this activity?

b Whenever something goes wrong in an organization, the first course of action is to explore the possibility of simple error. Once this has been ruled out, then it may be an idea to pose the question: Who looks guilty?

c Whenever something goes wrong in an organization, the first course of action is to set up in-house surveillance. Once this has been ruled out, then it may be an idea to pose the question: Who benefits from this activity?

d Whenever something goes wrong in an organization, the first course of action is to explore the possibility of simple error. Once this has been ruled out then it may be an idea to pose the question: Who benefits from this activity?

65 Which is the least appropriate statement?
Even if there is some benefit to be gained from taking a deceitful course of action and the employee can access the system or transaction in question, fraud will not necessarily occur.

a The employee will need to be motivated to commit fraud for fraud to happen.

b Motivation is about employees feeling that they have to resort to fraud as there are no other options left.

c Because these motives often relate to financial burdens, some organizations have installed staff counselling facilities where employees can ask for help with financial management or even short-term loans where they experience difficulties that they simply cannot resolve.

d Other organizations undertake regular credit scoring checks to make sure that employees who have access to company funds and who fail these checks are dismissed.

66 Insert the missing word.
If employees want to commit fraud and they have the means to do so, things start to get scary and problems may well arise. The next ingredient relates to . . . ., or what we can call the art of not getting caught.

a dishonesty

b concealment

c accessing

d greed

67 Insert the missing words.
   The reality of business life is that . . . ., so that
   someone owns the net worth of a business along with its income
   less expenditure. Where there is a gap due to fraud this equation
   will not add up, unless the records are in some way fudged to
   conceal the fraudulent deed.
   a assets will always equal liabilities
   b assets will always equal resources
   c loans will always equal liabilities
   d assets will never equal liabilities

68 Insert the missing figure.
   More than . . . . of fraudsters in our study had never previously
   been charged or convicted for a fraud-related offence.
   a 5%
   b 100%
   c 85%
   d 50%

69 Which is the most appropriate statement?
   a 10% of all frauds in this study were committed by employees in
      six departments: accounting, operations, sales, executive/upper
      management, customer service and purchasing.
   b 80% of all frauds in this study were committed by employees in
      two departments: accounting and operations.
   c 80% of all frauds in this study were committed by employees in
      two departments: customer service and purchasing.
   d 80% of all frauds in this study were committed by employees in
      six departments: accounting, operations, sales, executive/upper
      management, customer service and purchasing.

70 Which is the least appropriate statement?
   Pressures to commit fraud can comprise a wide variety of factors,
   such as:
   a Gambling, drugs, alcohol and other addictions causing financial
      stress.
   b Pressure from peer groups to adopt a lavish lifestyle that involves
      spending or investing large amounts of money.
   c Financial pressures due to health problems, impoverished friends
      and relatives and accumulated personal debt.
   d Career plans that are agreed with the line manager.

71 What is being referred to in this paragraph?

This most interesting concept has been used by criminologists for some time. We can view it as the ability to convince oneself that something that most people deem dishonest can be justified because there is a pressing need to take urgent action over and above the desire to remain honest.

a explanation
b rationalization
c improvisation
d notification

72 Which is the most appropriate statement?

a The bottom line is that notwithstanding any dire financial need, nothing illegal will happen 99% of the time and all is well. However, if the right set of circumstances come together at the right time, then illegality will be the most probable result.

b The bottom line is that notwithstanding any dire financial need, nothing illegal will happen 10% of the time and all is well. However, if the right set of circumstances come together at the right time, then illegality will be the most probable result.

c The bottom line is that notwithstanding any dire financial need, nothing illegal will happen 99% of the time and all is well. However, if the right set of circumstances come together at the right time, then illegality will be a slim probability.

d The bottom line is that notwithstanding any dire financial need, nothing illegal will happen 50% of the time and all is well. However, if the right set of circumstances come together at the right time, then illegality will be the most probable result.

73 Insert the missing word.

Occupational frauds are much more likely to be detected by . . . . than by any other means. This finding has been consistent since 2002 when we began tracking data on fraud detection methods.

a auditors
b managers
c tips-offs
d chance

74 Which is the most appropriate statement?
  a Fraudsters exhibit behavioural warning signs of their misdeeds. These green flags – such as living beyond one's means or exhibiting control issues – will not be identified by traditional controls.
  b Fraudsters exhibit behavioural warning signs of their misdeeds. These red flags – such as living with criminals or exhibiting control issues – will not be identified by traditional controls.
  c Fraudsters exhibit behavioural warning signs of their misdeeds. These red flags – such as living beyond one's means or exhibiting control issues – will be identified by traditional controls.
  d Fraudsters exhibit behavioural warning signs of their misdeeds. These red flags – such as living beyond one's means or exhibiting control issues – will not be identified by traditional controls.

75 Insert the missing words.
  Having . . . . could suggest that an illegal source of funds has been exploited.
  a savings
  b lots of money
  c a bank account
  d new clothes

76 Which is the most appropriate statement?
  a Lifestyle signals do have to be read carefully, but there is still a need to question someone who demonstrates a lifestyle that does not fit with what is generally known about this person.
  b Lifestyle hobbies do have to be read carefully, but there is still a need to question someone who demonstrates a lifestyle that does not fit with what is generally known about this person.
  c Lifestyle signals do have to be read carefully, but there is still a need to question someone who demonstrates a lifestyle that does not fit with their social class.
  d Eating habits do have to be read carefully, but there is still a need to question someone who demonstrates a lifestyle that does not fit with what is generally known about this person.

77 Which is the least appropriate statement?
  Research indicates that more senior people can do much more damage and for longer periods because of their position at work. We can also note that:

a A tried-and-trusted senior manager will tend to have a great deal of authority to approve transactions and alter records simply because of their special position.

b Where the fraud is high-level financial misstatement through inflating earnings, misreporting expenditure or hiding capital financing from the balance sheet to show misleading results, this can only be done by a few powerful executives.

c Managers in positions where they can override controls do not pose a serious threat.

d If there is someone in the organization who has always been responsible for an entire set of transactions, they may be able to access a system or a resource with no questions asked.

78 Insert the missing words.
When someone . . . ., this could be the result of many different reasons, for example they might be simply awkward and that is that. Or it could be that their behaviour is designed to distract or even stop anyone from examining their activities and finding out that something is wrong.

a works very hard
b behaves in an unusual manner
c performs poorly
d dislikes their boss

79 Which is the most appropriate statement?
   a If a staff member starts work early, leaves early and does not want any cover when they have to take time off, this may be to ensure that no one gets involved in their work area.

   b If a staff member starts work early, works late and does not want any cover when they have to take time off, this may be to ensure that no one gets involved in their personal affairs.

   c If a staff member starts work early, works late and does not want any cover when they have to take time off, this will certainly be to ensure that no one gets involved in their work area.

   d If a staff member starts work early, works late and does not want any cover when they have to take time off, this may be to ensure that no one gets involved in their work area.

80 Which is the least appropriate statement?
   Red flags can also include:
   a missing files and altered records.
   b close friendship groups at work.
   c odd journal transfers and photocopies in files.
   d unusual patterns of transactions.

PART V
Mastering Suitable Controls

Learning Objective

To describe an integrated fraud risk management process that allows you to assume a Fraud Smart approach to work.

17
The Control Concept

We are now on the final part of the book. The earlier parts were about the threat of fraud and how to recognize it at work. We can start to get much more proactive now as we look at some ways in which fraud can be controlled.

As you are aware, this book is based around the Fraud Smart cycle, which covers five key aspects of helping non-specialists get to grips with fraud at work. This is repeated in Figure 17.1.

This chapter sits within the fifth part of the Fraud Smart cycle, Mastering Suitable Controls, and covers the control concept as a way of managing the risk of fraud.

WHAT CAN GO WRONG?

The next chapter deals with some of the controls that most organizations use to ensure that they can achieve their goals and protect their resources. This chapter takes a step back and considers a well-known control model that serves as a platform on which specific controls can be built. If we fail to get this platform right, much could go wrong.

We can consider the way in which problems can arise by looking at a brief illustrative case study taken from the UK:

Figure 17.1 The Fraud Smart cycle.

CASE STUDY

An accounts clerk plundered £630 000 from her employer to fund a luxury lifestyle. She also told her bosses that she was suffering from cancer so she could take time off to have cosmetic surgery. Her crime spree began when she gained access to the electronic wage list. The trusted clerk appeared dedicated and received salary rises, but nevertheless began to invent fake employees for her own financial gain. Over the next five years she paid wages into false accounts. After the business suffered significant cash-flow problems and had to lay off 26 staff, her boss started asking her questions about the finances. As the net began to close, she went off sick and used a bogus CV to join a rival firm, from which she stole £3535.

WHAT DO THE EXPERTS SAY?

The first principle of *Managing the Business Risk of Fraud* sets out the need to manage the threat of fraud:

> As part of an organization's governance structure, a fraud risk management program should be in place, including a written policy

(or policies) to convey the expectations of the board of directors and senior management regarding managing fraud risk. (MBRF, page 6)

Sound controls are a significant part of the way in which fraud can be managed and without sound controls there will be problems, as identified by the Association of Certified Fraud Examiners:

> To further examine the unique challenges faced by small businesses, we compared internal control weaknesses at organizations with fewer than 100 employees to those at larger organizations. The small organizations had a noted deficiency in internal controls that allowed fraud to occur. In nearly half of the cases at small companies, a lack of internal controls was cited as the factor that most contributed to the occurrence of the fraud. Control overrides were markedly less common at small companies than at their larger counterparts, most likely because the lack of controls in so many small organizations meant there was nothing to override. (ACFE Report, page 45)

MBRF makes it quite clear that preventive controls are really important:

> Prevention is the most proactive fraud-fighting measure. The design and implementation of control activities should be a coordinated effort spearheaded by management with an assembled cast of employees. Collectively, this cross section of the organization should be able to address all of the identified risks, design and implement the control activities, and ensure that the techniques used are adequate to prevent fraud from occurring in accordance with the organization's risk tolerance. (MBRF, page 30)

OUR MODEL EXPLAINED

We have developed a simple model in Figure 17.2 to illustrate one way of dealing with the issues raised in this chapter.

Our model suggests that there are five tenets of good control that will underpin how specific controls are designed and applied within an organization. This framework is an adaptation of a well-known model that has been in existence for many years, known as the Committee of Sponsoring Organizations (COSO) control framework. Some commentators have argued that this framework is becoming somewhat dated, but it still holds sway in terms of being applicable to most larger

Figure 17.2   The control concept.

organizations. While we have made a few changes to the standard framework, its essence remains. Note that the COSO website (www. coso.org) has a great deal of information that may be useful.

We can explore the framework by considering each separate part of our model in turn.

Control Environment

The control environment is what some writers call the 'tone at the top', which sets the agenda for good control and the standards of conduct that are detailed in the code of ethics:

- The tone at the top is also set by the corporate policies that come from the board. Values, standards, recruitment and performance measures will together reinforce a culture that either promotes good controls or leaves much to chance.
- The control environment provides a view on tolerance and whether compliance is seen as a major issue, as well as whether people are allowed to be reckless or need to judge the impact of their decisions

carefully before they are implemented. Some people call this tension between degrees of control the 'risk appetite'.

- The main point to grasp is that fraud may or may not happen, but to guard against it, fixed controls should be in place. Everyone in the organization needs to adhere to the rules, as a 'free-for-all' culture can easily mask dishonesty.
- Moreover, controls cost money and tend to slow things down. If an agent has to get decisions approved by a more senior person, this means that a deal can become stalled until it is signed off – while the new customer may get frustrated and threaten to walk away from the deal. Nevertheless, if no approval is required the sales agent could plant a false account in the system or engage in money laundering.

It is the control environment that sets standards on acceptable behaviour and tensions between tight controls and allowing people to do their job and make decisions. Many commentators argue that the board should detail a risk appetite that says how the balance between control and risk should be perceived. The reality is that this concept of risk appetite means different things to different people and has to be seen as different degrees of risk taking being allowed, depending on the person, team, business line and priorities within the organization. That means that the risk appetite will vary in different parts of an organization depending on the range of factors that the board feels are important. For fraud risks, the control environment will ask: What is our civic duty on employee fraud and to what extent can we install sufficient measures to ensure that it never happens?

Risk Assessment

Our model goes in a cycle that starts with the control environment and then comes to risk assessment. Here the risk of fraud needs to be ascertained and checked out; that is, it needs to be assessed:

- Risk assessment is about looking at each work area in question and judging to what extent fraud could occur.
- The idea is that those closest to the action should do this assessment, which means that each manager and work team will want to understand the fraud risks that affect them and then weigh them up to judge which are the most dangerous.

We discuss this issue of risk management in later chapters. At this stage we can simply say that the threat of fraud needs to be very carefully assessed in terms of known frauds, emerging frauds and those more complex ones that may possibly arise if controls fail to counter them. For fraud risks, the risk assessment stage will ask: Do we know enough about potential fraud and is there anything lurking out there that we do not know about?

Controls

We have considered the context in terms of the overall control environment and assessed fraud risks. Now specific controls can be devised or existing ones reviewed to address the threat of these potential frauds. The control strategy asks that each stage of the cycle is worked through so that the controls that are designed or refined fit the bill; that is, they address the current state of the risks that exist and are in danger of undermining the resources entrusted to each management team.

We are not going to go into too much detail here, as the battery of controls that are available to fight fraud and abuse are dealt with in the next chapter. For now, it is enough to say that according to the COSO model, controls should fit the risks against which they guard. So controls should:

- Prevent significant fraud from ever happening.
- Detect any frauds that, despite our best efforts, have still pierced our defences.
- Respond to such a fraud by cleaning up the damage, dealing with the culprit, recovering lost funds and tightening up weak controls that allowed the fraud to happen in the first place.

Controls are there to help manage risk and help bring the potential impact of fraud down to an acceptable level. For fraud risks, the control response will ask: Are our controls sharp enough to combat the ever-changing types of fraud that are out there and can they be overriden at all?

Monitoring

Each organization will have its own control environment, and the anti-fraud strategy will form a major part of fraud control. Both management and staff will be working hard to identify fraud risks and to ensure that the controls are fit for purpose. Note the following:

- In one sense the activity should end there, but for larger organizations the idea of monitoring is very important as an additional feature of business life. This is because the concept of governance that we discussed in Chapter 1 means that managers have to report back to the owners and other stakeholders on how they are doing, including tackling possible fraud and corruption.
- Monitoring is partly about reviewing controls and making sure that the COSO cycle is working well. However, it is also about giving assurances that all is well. So monitoring is not just having a look at the way fraud is managed, it can also be a formal process for checking and reporting back that each management team is fulfilling the corporate policy on fraud control.
- It is possible to ask the internal auditors to do regular reviews of the way controls have been sharpened up by managers, although this will have to fit into their audit plan, which means that it cannot cover all teams, every year, across the entire organization. The auditors will prioritize their audit work based on a careful assessment of relative risk.

For fraud risks, the monitoring stage sits firmly with management, who need to ask: To what extent can we tell our stakeholders that we have fraud under control and are on a constant watch for any new scams?

Objectives, Information and Communication

We have changed the standard COSO model to place business objectives right in the middle of the cycle, driven by information and communication systems that should run across the entire organization:

- Controls must be driven by the agreed business objectives, as the idea of control is to help ensure that objectives are fully achieved.
- The whole point of this book is to create more awareness of fraud risk and ways to respond to this risk for people within an organization who have no specialized knowledge of fraud. That means that risk issues and various responses to the changing nature of the threat should be on the board's corporate radar and be part of head office business priorities as well as local team agendas.

- There is no way a management team in a local area office should be embarking on a fraud risk review without linking into the way this is done across the entire organization as a crucial part of managing business processes.
- Newsletters, workshops, corporate guidance and facilitation are all part of how the organization can communicate with its members about fraud control. Reports on activities and the latest threats should be disseminated by the anti-fraud experts on a regular basis.

A final weapon is fraud awareness training, as a great way of spreading the way in which managers and staff are dealing with this issue across different business lines and support teams. For fraud risks, this part of our model asks: Do our people know enough about the anti-fraud policy and strategy to ensure that they build fraud control into how they achieve their business goals?

OUR THREE KEY CONCLUSIONS

Controls are so crucial that there is a need to stand back and think about a formal framework before launching into the basic control mechanisms. That is what we have done in this chapter. Setting the framework is part of the corporate direction from the main board, which should be aligned to the anti-fraud strategy.

There are three main conclusions that we can draw from our discussions and suggestions in this chapter. These conclusions will be used to drive your Fraud Smart toolkit, which you will be designing at the end of this part of the book:

17.1 The board should ensure that fraud control is a key part of the overall control framework and that it fits with the main components, which in our case use the well-known COSO format.
17.2 Each management team should ensure that it is reviewing fraud risk and associated controls on a regular basis to discharge its role in the anti-fraud policy.
17.3 Efforts to establish fraud control cycles should be monitored for effectiveness and each manager will want to share any appropriate information and advice across all business lines.

We said in the Preface that everyone who works for or is associated with a larger organization should appreciate what fraud is and its ramifications. One way of making sure that these ramifications are addressed is to monitor fraud control continuously as part of the wider business risk management process.

18
Basic Controls

We had a look at control frameworks in the previous chapter and now we need to examine some of the basic controls that are available for combating fraud and abuse.

As you are aware, this book is based around the Fraud Smart cycle, which covers five key aspects of helping non-specialists get to grips with fraud at work. This is repeated in Figure 18.1.

This chapter sits within the fifth part of the Fraud Smart cycle, Mastering Suitable Controls, and covers basic controls that can be used as standard mechanisms for fraud control.

WHAT CAN GO WRONG?

Everything we have said in the previous chapters of this book has established the context for fraud control. What is most important is to get the controls in and to make sure that they actually work. If we fail to install controls that can deal with the so-called trusted manager, who actually cannot be trusted, so much could go wrong.

We can consider how problems can arise by looking at two brief illustrative case studies taken from the UK and the USA. The first trusted manager worked in the construction industry:

Figure 18.1   The Fraud Smart cycle.

CASE STUDY

A trusted construction manager for a plumbing and heating firm spent five years defrauding the company. He was responsible for managing construction jobs, which meant that he purchased supplies and provided documentation to support the payment of these goods. He would add other materials to official purchase orders and receive personal payments for the materials he provided for his friends, which were paid for by the company. An accounts clerk covering stock control discovered discrepancies with supplier invoices.

A basic control ensuring that no one can operate a process that involves resources in isolation from others can help avoid a recipe for fraud:

CASE STUDY

A former school facilities director was sentenced to two years and nine months in federal prison for stealing more than half a million dollars from the school. The defendant pleaded guilty to felony crimes of mail fraud and tax evasion and was ordered to repay $652 000 to the high school and $170 000 to the Internal Revenue Service. It was alleged that he was a trusted employee who worked long hours and rarely took time off, but that on over 90 occasions he submitted phoney invoices to the school that were sent out by a company he owned, and he also personally approved those same invoices as part of a scheme to divert school funds fraudulently to his accounts. As facilities manager he had complete authority to approve repair invoices of up to $1500 without approval of other officials; anything above this had to be approved by the principal, who trusted the facilities manager and so saw no reason to question the invoices.

WHAT DO THE EXPERTS SAY?

Our first quote from our key texts is a well-timed warning that controls cannot guard against all frauds all the time:

> Internal controls alone are insufficient to fully prevent occupational fraud. Though it is important for organizations to have strategic and effective anti-fraud controls in place, internal controls will not prevent all fraud from occurring, nor will they detect most fraud once it begins. (ACFE Report 2010, page 5)

Having said that, sound internal controls are still really important. *Managing the Business Risk of Fraud*'s principle 3 argues that preventive techniques are important in avoiding key fraud risks in the first place, even if they cannot guarantee zero frauds:.

> Despite the best efforts of those responsible for preventing fraud, one inevitable reality remains: 'fraud happens.' Because fraud and misconduct can occur at various levels in any organization, it is essential that appropriate preventive and detective techniques are in place. Although fraud prevention and detection are related concepts, they are not the same. While prevention encompasses policies, procedures, training, and communication, detection involves activities and programs designed to identify fraud or misconduct that is occurring or has occurred. Although preventive measures cannot ensure that fraud will not be committed, they are the first line of defense in minimizing fraud risk. (MBRF, page 30)

Principle 4 suggests that detection techniques should be in place to uncover fraud events when preventive measures have failed:

> Every organization is susceptible to fraud, but not all fraud can be prevented, nor is it cost-effective to try. An organization may determine it is more cost-effective to design its controls to detect, rather than prevent, certain fraud schemes. It is important that organizations consider both fraud prevention and fraud detection. (MBRF, page 9)

OUR MODEL EXPLAINED

We have developed a simple model in Figure 18.2 to illustrate one way of dealing with the issues raised in this chapter.

Our model suggests that there are several well-known mechanisms for combating the threat of fraud and that as the threat alters, the way in which these mechanisms are employed should be adjusted accordingly. We need to make one crucial point before we can go through the model, however. These control mechanisms are basic ways of tackling fraud,

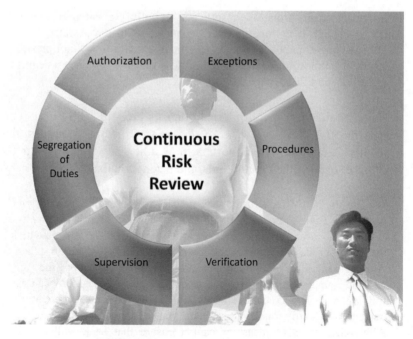

Figure 18.2 Types of basic controls.

and for that matter business risks generally. For very specific fraud threats the managers for the area in question will need to design specific controls that fit the bill. For example, a bank may place flags on credit card transactions that fall outside the normal range, say a large transaction from a foreign country. These controls are built for very precise threats and it would be impossible to develop a list of such unique anti-fraud measures, as it would run into hundreds of pages of detailed text.

In this chapter, we explore some of the basic controls by considering each separate part of our model in turn.

Authorization

Authorization is the simple act of making sure that everything that happens in an organization is supposed to happen; that is, that the activity fits the criteria for what have been agreed as official activities approved by management:

- Each employee operates as an agent for their employer and should have a set level of authority in terms of how they represent their employer to the outside world.
- The vast majority of frauds relate to activity that has not been approved. It is only where an entire organization engages in fraudulent behaviour, say by regularly overcharging its clients for work done, that it could be argued that the inflated charges were actually authorized. The counter-argument is that management cannot authorize anything that is in fact illegal.
- Most authorization processes are aligned to the management structure, so that the more material and high risk the item, the more attention it gets from senior management before it is approved.
- Authorization is also related to systems access rights, which should be reviewed on a regular basis, particularly when staff change roles within an organization.
- Another aspect of authorization is to ensure that there are full audit trails logging transactions all the way through a system and to assign unique identities for all activity carried out by staff members.

When considering ways of tackling unauthorized activity, the question to ask is: How can we ensure that this type of transaction does not make it through our systems?

Exceptions

Having exceptions is both a preventive control, in that it deters employees from attempting suspect transactions, and a detective control that will hopefully pick up suspect items that have got through despite the organization's best efforts:

- Strong organizations run exception-reporting routines on a continuous basis. So long as we know what to look for, problems may be intercepted. Unfortunately, new frauds can get around exception reports by making sure that the activity looks and feels 'normal'.
- Proactive data analysis (or data mining) can look for relationships between different data that should not exist, say an employee's mobile phone number appearing on supporting documents from a building company for a large and complex contract. These exception tests can be run on an ongoing basis.
- The explanations for many exceptions may be quite simple, but each should be probed to make sure that what is being said is in fact the case. Intrusion-detection software will look for suspicious traffic over the corporate network based on comparing normal with unusual patterns.

The key question to ask is: How can we best pick up suspect or incorrect activities through our system tools and checking routines?

Procedures

Procedures cover just about everything that occurs in an organization that needs to happen in a set manner:

- Procedures are there to ensure a consistent response to transactions, enquiries, orders, projects, new developments, recruiting staff, training, performance appraisal, planning, marketing products, researching new ventures – the list goes on and on.
- So the security procedures will guard against unauthorized access that puts resources at risk. Securing IT systems may mean using an international or industry standard and adopting the protocols required by this standard.
- Ongoing staff vetting (along with credit checks and criminal records checks) will be handled through a procedure that seeks to make sure staff are reliable through checking arrangements that are accelerated

to fit the nature of the staff group and risks of fraud inherent in that role.

- This procedure will have to compete with data privacy rules that are designed to protect personal data, some of which may be needed to do the staff vetting. Privacy protection itself is designed to prevent fraud, abuse and violation of human rights. The differences can be reconciled where the vetting is reasonable and disclosed to the workforce so that everyone knows what to expect.
- Effective procedures for budgetary control and asset accounting can all be used to ensure good control over resources and how they are used.

The key question to ask is: Do the procedures work in ensuring that the risk of fraud is minimized?

Verification

Verification is a key control over fraud and abuse. This is about checking that the representation of something is what it purports to be:

- Fraud can happen when someone or something slips through the net. Double checking is a good way of trying to stop this happening. Identity verification is crucial to stop frauds such as money laundering, where several different types of original documents are required to make sure that the identity of the person in question is valid.
- Verification systems are so important that they should be subject to a separate compliance routine in high-risk companies such as banks and insurance companies.
- A well-known concept is to trust everyone but to verify everything.

The key question to ask is: Is this person the same as they say they are – how can we be sure?

Supervision

Managers have to keep an eye on their staff and supervisors need to monitor their team members if their respective roles in fraud control are to work:

- Supervision is mainly about performance issues, but can also be used to make sure that people are able to stay in line with standards of conduct and the way set procedures are operated.

- Supervision is important where staff are dealing with high-risk areas such as cash, accounting records, contract negotiations, overseas permits, software engineering and a whole range of high-risk parts of the business.

The question to ask is: Are these high-risk areas adequately supervised?

Segregation of Duties

The final basic control concept relates to segregation of duties (SoD):

- The idea is to ensure that no one person has an excessive amount of control over transactions, resources or decisions to ensure that they cannot embark on fraud without colluding with others. It also means that they will not readily be able to conceal a fraud.
- SoD is also related to clear role definitions and privilege/access rules across the organization. This comes about through formal organizational groupings, where boundaries of responsibilities, authority levels and reporting lines are set in a way that copes with work teams as well as flexible resources.
- The basic idea of SoD is to separate ordering or initiating a transaction from custody of the benefits, paying for the item and accounting for it.

The key question for this control is: How can we ensure that employees do not have an excessive degree of influence over high-risk areas of the business, which makes the prospect of fraud more likely to arise and easier to conceal?

OUR THREE KEY CONCLUSIONS

We are getting closer to being able to tackle fraud. The overall control framework was outlined in the previous chapter, and we have now profiled some of the basic controls for helping organizations handle risk, including the risk of fraud.

There are three main conclusions that we can draw from our discussions and suggestions in this chapter. These conclusions will be used to drive your Fraud Smart toolkit, which you will be designing at the end of this part of the book:

18.1 Everyone should appreciate the dynamics of controls that safeguard against fraud with a view to preventing and detecting potential and actual fraud and abuse.
18.2 Everyone should be aware of the limitations of controls that mean that they cannot be relied on to prevent all frauds all the time.
18.3 Everyone should be able to understand and work with basic controls that guard against fraud and appreciate the way in which these controls work in practice.

The main response to the threat of fraud is to use all the basic controls that are available to manage the threat and then to design unique controls to deal with any remaining threats. This idea of Fraud Smart risk management is explored in some more detail in the next chapter.

19
Fraud Smart Risk Management

We are coming towards the end of this book and there is a need to pull everything together in this slightly longer chapter, where we examine the overarching concept of fraud risk management.

As you are aware, this book is based around the Fraud Smart cycle, which covers five key aspects of helping non-specialists get to grips with fraud at work. This is repeated in Figure 19.1.

This chapter sits within the fifth part of the Fraud Smart cycle, Mastering Suitable Controls, and covers the way in which the typical business risk management used by most organizations can incorporate fraud risks to provide a comprehensive framework for dealing with fraud.

WHAT CAN GO WRONG?

The growing threat of fraud is often overlooked in many organizations and this is not helped by the fact that some managers may not buy into the view that they are responsible for managing this threat. What is needed is a way of integrating fraud risk into and inside the more usual business risks with which most managers are used to dealing. If we fail to get this integration, much could go wrong.

We can consider how problems can arise by looking at two brief illustrative case studies taken from the UK and the USA, the first at a supermarket:

Figure 19.1   The Fraud Smart cycle.

CASE STUDY

A former IT manager at a large supermarket was given a 20-month jail term after stealing over £81 000 worth of loyalty points from the retailer. He stole 17 million loyalty points and credited them to various accounts using false names. He then used the reward points to buy thousands of pounds worth of goods from the store. When confronted about the fraud he was working as a lead analyst programmer and he said, 'I discovered a loophole in the system. There wasn't a proper check in place. I was a trusted employee so no one was looking over my shoulder.' The judge told the manager, 'You had access to the loyalty card scheme. You abused your position over a period of years by putting points on to false cards. It is clear your initial motive was greed. This was a carefully planned, well-worked fraud.' The IT manager was sentenced to 20 months in prison for the fraud and ordered to repay the amounts defrauded from the company.

Where there is the real risk of fraud, this risk must be countered by effective controls such as good procedures, segregation of duties and supervisory oversight:

CASE STUDY

A defendant pleaded guilty to four counts of mail fraud and four counts of filing false federal income tax returns. This previously trusted executive assistant of a car parts distributor received a sentence of 68 months in prison followed by three years' probation for the embezzlement of more than $1.4 million from her employer. She was ordered to pay back $1.3 million to the company and its insurer, as well as back taxes, penalties and fees to the Internal Revenue Service. A criminal records check also revealed that this was the defendant's third conviction for embezzlement from an employer. She had held various positions at the company, including administrative assistant to the president and director of human resources. Her duties and responsibilities had included sales and marketing, accounting, human resources and merchandising, and she had had authority to approve and sign purchase orders, invoices and cheques for less than $85 000, if these matters were in the normal course of business. According to court records, the defendant created a fictitious business entity to facilitate a fraudulent scheme. For approximately nine years, she defrauded her employer by generating fictitious invoices and submitting them to her employer for payment. Since she had authority to approve the purchase orders and cheques, she would approve these phoney invoices and ultimately transfer the funds into her personal bank accounts. The money was used to pay for her son's college tuition, to finance frequent trips abroad and to completely redesign her home.

WHAT DO THE EXPERTS SAY?

Managing the Business Risk of Fraud gets straight to the point by making a firm suggestion on fraud risk management:

> To protect itself and its stakeholders effectively and efficiently from fraud, an organization should understand fraud risk and the specific risks that directly or indirectly apply to the organization. A structured fraud risk assessment, tailored to the organization's size, complexity, industry, and goals, should be performed and updated periodically. The assessment may be integrated with an overall organizational risk assessment or performed as a stand-alone exercise, but should, at a minimum, include risk identification, risk likelihood and significance assessment, and risk response. (MBRF, page 7)

MBRF goes on to warn about the frauds that can be perpetrated by the senior executives as they stuggle to survive in volatile markets where investors demand strong returns:

> An effective fraud risk identification process includes an assessment of the incentives, pressures, and opportunities to commit fraud. Employee incentive programs and the metrics on which they are based can provide a map to where fraud is most likely to occur. Fraud risk assessment should consider the potential override of controls by management as well as areas where controls are weak or there is a lack of segregation of duties. (MBRF, page 8)

One further piece of guidance, while pretty short, contains a great deal of crucial material:

> Assessing the likelihood and significance of each potential fraud risk is a subjective process that should consider not only monetary significance, but also significance to an organization's financial reporting, operations, and reputation, as well as legal and regulatory compliance requirements. An initial assessment of fraud risk should consider the inherent risk of a particular fraud in the absence of any known controls that may address the risk. Individual organizations will have different risk tolerances. (MBRF, page 8)

The overall advice is to assess risk across the board and look for fraud risks that do not have suitable controls to address their consequences. The guide also refers to the complex concept of risk tolerances and the fact that different organizations will have different acceptable levels. Getting staff together and asking them to think about the risk of fraud and what can be done about it is one useful approach described by our experts:

> Once assembled, the risk assessment team should go through a brain-storming activity to identify the organization's fraud risks. Effective brainstorming involves preparation in advance of the meeting, a leader to set the agenda and facilitate the session, and openness to ideas regarding potential risks and controls. Brainstorming enables discussions of the incentives, pressures, and opportunities to commit fraud; risks of management override of controls; and the population of fraud risks relevant to the organization. Other risks, such as regulatory and legal misconduct and reputation risk, as well as the impact of IT on fraud risks also should be considered in the fraud risk identification process. (MBRF, page 22)

Our final quote calls for a structured rather than a haphazard approach to the task of ensuring effective fraud risk management:

> Fraud risks can be addressed by establishing practices and controls to mitigate the risk, accepting the risk – but monitoring actual exposure – or designing ongoing or specific fraud evaluation procedures to deal with individual fraud risks. An organization should strive for a structured approach versus a haphazard approach. (MBRF page 8)

OUR MODEL EXPLAINED

We have developed a simple model in Figure 19.2 to illustrate one way of dealing with the issues raised in this chapter.

Our final model suggests a way of bringing together all the issues and topics that have been discussed in earlier chapters of the book. The model is held together by the concept of enterprise risk management, which makes sure that risk-based steps to improve controls and promote

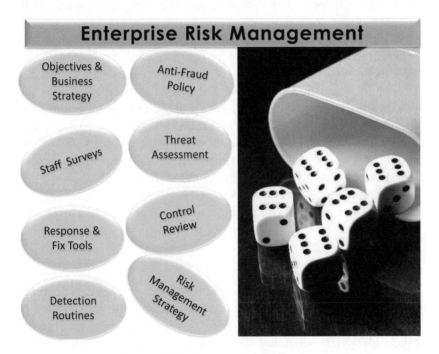

Figure 19.2 Fraud risk management.

success are brought together through a structured rather than haphazard approach to this task.

We can explore these issues by considering each separate part of our model in turn.

Objectives and Business Strategy

We start our model with the objectives and business strategy with which the organization is currently working. This approach is aimed at countering the basic problem with anti-fraud measures: most people feel that they are not related to their role in seeking to achieve business goals. They are seen as 'nice-to-have' rather than 'must-have' measures.

The best way to deal with fraud and abuse is to relate it to business goals. Each organization will have set goals that it needs to achieve and will have to report back to stakeholders on how it is getting on. If the goals are based on wide-ranging concepts that adopt a long-term focus, making sure that ethics is at the centre of everything and that the corporate reputation is protected and enhanced, then it is easy to see where fraud risk management fits in. Where objectives are linked only to short-term income targets, there is less incentive to engage in fraud risk assessment.

As part of the overall business objectives in achieving set goals and growing the business, it is necessary to align risk management with this task, because risks are things that get in the way of achieving objectives. As such, it is a good idea to have a strategy for making sure that the fraud risk management process makes a proper contribution to achieving success by engineering what we have called a Fraud Smart culture. The fraud risk efforts should therefore flow from the business strategy by arguing that success can only happen within a culture that promotes honesty and tackles dishonesty within the workforce.

A risk log can be developed to record responses to known risks, but this must start with business objectives. Figure 19.3 is a simple illustration.

Anti-Fraud Policy

We can now move forwards from the business strategy to the anti-fraud policy and strategy. The anti-fraud policy will ask the organization to define its view on fraud and how this view is expressed to its stakeholders. The anti-fraud strategy will include all the usual items, including such topics as:

Business objectives: Deliver £3m of quality e-learning to client X in 20xx				Line manager: XYZ Business Unit		
INHERENT RISKS	IMPACT OF THESE RISKS	HOW LIKELY THEY ARE	EXISTING CONTROLS	IMPROVEMENT REQUIRED	BY WHOM	BY WHEN

Figure 19.3   Simplified risk log 1.

- Policy aim and ownership, board approval and review process.
- Board's role and involvement.
- Roles and responsibilities across the organization.
- Fraud reporting channels.
- Data mining and other fraud-detection tools.
- Risk assessment and ongoing threat analysis.
- Fraud proofing new developments and new policy initiatives.
- Specific measures such as security, staff vetting and conflict of interest procedures and visitor access.
- Personal screening of staff, agents, associates and customers.
- Sharing information with partners and law enforcement agencies.
- Staff surveys on fraud awareness levels and whether management is doing a good job in fraud control.
- Fraud awareness seminars and online resources.
- Staff identification procedures, along with badges, CCTV, official uniforms, search routines and personal lockers.
- Fraud risk workshops and resulting team-level risk register.
- How to promote a Fraud Smart culture where prevention, detection and response are addressed by everyone.

Over and above the coverage in the fraud policy, a great anti-fraud measure is simply to insert a few lines from the policy on the risk log, to ensure that the workforce addresses fraud as a business risk, as in Figure 19.4.

Business objectives: Deliver £3m of quality e-learning to client X in 20xx				Line manager: XYZ Business Unit		
INHERENT RISKS	IMPACT OF THESE RISKS	HOW LIKELY THEY ARE	EXISTING CONTROLS	IMPROVEMENT REQUIRED	BY WHOM	BY WHEN
EXTRACT FROM THE ANTI-FRAUD POLICY:	*'Whenever the risk log is updated by the business lines and business support teams, the threat of existing and emerging frauds should be incorporated within the risk assessments and ensuing risk management strategies.'*					

Figure 19.4   Simplified risk log 2.

Threat Assessment

Effective fraud risk management has a pivotal focus on threat assessment. The logic is simple: if an organization is able to identify all the different types of fraud and security breaches it could suffer, it can then make sure that each threat is countered through a set of solid corporate defence mechanisms that will protect it. If successful threat assessment can be done, then, in general, all will be well. The realities of corporate life are not so simple, however. It is not possible to lock down everything in an organization, nor is it possible to intall a security regime such that managers and staff are not able to make decisions or approve daily transactions without first reporting to a panel of senior security officers who would examine every detail.

Threat assessment must be built into the way the organization and its people carry out their business as a natural way of working and getting the job done. In this scenario, threat assessment should be part of the ongoing process of looking at risks and emerging issues in which every manager is involved, before they are able to update their business risk management strategy. The idea is to work with colleagues and team members to ensure that a robust risk log is in place that also addresses fraud risks and sets out how controls may be improved to guard against risks to the achievement of business objectives. This is illustrated in Figure 19.5.

Business objectives: Deliver £3m of quality e-learning to client X in 20xx				Line manager: XYZ Business Unit		
INHERENT RISKS	**IMPACT OF THESE RISKS**	**HOW LIKELY THEY ARE**	**EXISTING CONTROLS**	**IMPROVEMENT REQUIRED**	**BY WHOM**	**BY WHEN**
Goes over budget	HIGH	LOW				
Copyright material is stolen	HIGH	HIGH				

Figure 19.5 Simplified risk log 3.

Control Review

We arrive next at control review, where controls need to be considered in terms of whether they can deal with the fraud risks that have been identified (Figure 19.6):

Business objectives: Deliver £3m of quality e-learning to client X in 20xx				Line manager: XYZ Business Unit		
INHERENT RISKS	**IMPACT OF THESE RISKS**	**HOW LIKELY THEY ARE**	**EXISTING CONTROLS**	**IMPROVEMENT REQUIRED**	**BY WHOM**	**BY WHEN**
Goes over budget	HIGH	LOW	Good budgetary control and monitoring			
Copyright material is stolen	HIGH	HIGH	None in place at present			

Figure 19.6 Simplified risk log 4.

Risk Management Strategy

The operational risk management strategy for the business unit in question may then be developed by going on to consider the overall approach to dealing with risks, including fraud risks, after having considered whether existing controls are working well or not. This is illustrated in Figure 19.7.

Business objectives: Deliver £3m of quality e-learning to client X in 20xx				Line manager: XYZ Business Unit		
INHERENT RISKS	IMPACT OF THESE RISKS	HOW LIKELY THEY ARE	EXISTING CONTROLS	IMPROVEMENT REQUIRED	BY WHOM	BY WHEN
Goes over budget	HIGH	LOW	Good budgetary control and monitoring	Keep budgetary system under review	B	Each quarter
Copyright material is stolen	HIGH	HIGH	None in place at present	Set up a rapid project to review security of e-learning resources	C	Report next month

Figure 19.7   Simplified risk log 5.

Detection Routines

So far we have put in place a risk management strategy that takes on board the need to respond to fraud risks by making sure that sound controls are in place, or if they are not by strengthening the existing controls. While this is good fraud risk management, it is still not enough. Because of the nature of deceit within fraud, we also need an ongoing search for concealed frauds that are happening undetected. This means that detection routines are an important part of the overall strategy (see Figure 19.8).

Business objectives:				Line manager:		
Deliver £3m of quality e-learning to client X in 20xx				XYZ Business Unit		
INHERENT RISKS	**IMPACT OF THESE RISKS**	**HOW LIKELY THEY ARE**	**EXISTING CONTROLS**	**IMPROVEMENT REQUIRED**	**BY WHOM**	**BY WHEN**
Goes over budget	HIGH	LOW	Good budgetary control and monitoring	Keep budgetary system under review	B	Each quarter
Copyright material is stolen	HIGH	HIGH	None in place at present	Set up project to review security of e-learning resources	C	Report next month
			1. Review Internet for examples of our e-learning material that has been cloned for resale. 2. Data mine employees for links with competitors' businesses		Anti-fraud team	Next week

Figure 19.8 Simplified risk log 6.

Response and Fix Tools

The next part of our Fraud Smart risk management cycle relates to providing an effective response to frauds that have actually arisen by considering the following topics:

- *Preliminary assessment.* As soon as a fraud comes to light, it is essential that the fraud response plan swings into action. This may well involve the legal team, human resources, the director for the area affected and the investigating team, which may be led by internal audit. The question to address is: Has a fraud actually happened?
- *Initial response and threat control.* The first response will involve making sure that the right people are informed, securing the evidence, ensuring confidentiality, looking for additional fraud threats as the picture emerges and fixing any controls that have failed.

- *Interim report.* A formal report should be drawn up dealing with the matters mentioned above for consideration by the key decision maker, which may be the relevant director with advice from legal. Progress on the investigation may be monitored by the audit committee. It may be possible to freeze bank accounts for the suspect(s) in question.
- *Investigation plan and police role.* An investigation team and lead investigator should be appointed and the police may be asked for a view on the case and whether they will be involved at this early stage of events.
- *The full investigation.* The main investigation will be carried out with a view to securing the available evidence and discovering the truth. The employee in question may be suspended if the evidence would otherwise be at risk. Or, on occasion, the investigation may start out as covert in order to secure live evidence if this is seen as the best way forward.
- *Securing evidence.* This is a crucial stage of an investigation that is about uncovering the truth and securing evidence that is sufficient, reliable and convincing enough to support subsequent charges using the rigorous standards of the criminal justice system. Tainted evidence is evidence that has lost its integrity, infringes the rights of the suspect or simply breaches the rules of evidence gathering set by criminal law, which means that it might get thrown out of court.
- *Interviewing.* Witnesses, colleagues, managers and others will be interviewed to secure evidence that supports the investigation by proving or disproving the allegations.
- *Confidentiality and media contact.* During the course of the investigation, regard will be paid to confidentiality and the way the media will be informed about events. It is best to use one channel of communication, say the press office, so as to control the proceedings and guard against defamation and excessive damage to the corporate reputation.
- *Action options.* The investigation will result in a report that will give direction about possible criminal proceedings and staff disciplinary procedures for gross misconduct. The disciplinary procedure may be based around breach of procedure and possible dismissal at an early stage, where there is sufficient evidence regarding the conduct of the employee. Meanwhile, the police case will focus on criminal charges and a conviction, which may take time to conclude.
- *Recovery.* Throughout the investigation, the question of recovery and damage limitation will be assessed, although offers for the return

of funds by the suspect will have to be discussed with the company lawyers.

- *Control fixes.* While the above investigation is progressing, management should be involved in fixing weaknesses in internal controls as part of the ongoing Fraud Smart risk management process.

The above is a very brief account of what some internal fraud investigations might look like. One crucial consideration is that Fraud Smart people should not be intimately involved in this type of work, which should be done by people trained in forensic examination. However, anyone may be called on to cooperate with an ongoing investigation.

Staff Surveys

Staff surveys are part of our model because it is necessary to try to measure the extent to which the workforce is Fraud Smart. It is a good idea to set a benchmark and assess on a regular basis how aware and alert employees at all levels are, and what progress has been made in this respect.

There are many different versions of surveys and some of the questions asked may cover areas such as the following:

- Are you aware of the anti-fraud policy?
- Have you received training in the last 12 months?
- How do you rate this training?
- Have you used the online e-learning resource in the last 12 months?
- How do you rate this e-learning resource?
- Are you aware of the red flags for fraud that would alert you to a possible fraud at work?
- Would you know what to do if you became aware of a fraud?
- Do you trust the whistleblowing process and feel it is worthwhile?
- Do you carry out regular risk management assessment in your work team?
- Does your work team build the threat of fraud into their business risk management assessments?
- Have you experienced any fraud or breach of procedure that you would like to discuss?

• Do you have any ideas for improving the way the organization manages the risk of fraud?

Enterprise Risk Management

ERM sits in the middle of our model. This is because it is an all-consuming process that sucks in risks from all parts of the organization and seeks to have these risks assessed and managed in a structured manner. The equation is quite straightforward and can be summed up in 10 simple tasks:

1 Have in place an integrated method for managing risk that is driven by the business strategy adopted, which is there to drive success through the organization.
2 Take ownership of fraud risk management by being Fraud Smart.
3 Adopt a zero tolerance of fraud based on the adopted code of business ethics and state that it should not be allowed to happen here or there will be stiff consequences.
4 Make sure that the threat of fraud is assessed in a rigorous and dynamic manner.
5 Build the threat of fraud into the way business risk is assessed and managed through the enterprise-wide process.
6 Improve controls, tighten loopholes and do not base controls on the assumption that everyone is trustworthy at all times.
7 Check that people are complying with controls.
8 Talk to your staff about fraud risk management and train them to be Fraud Smart.
9 Keep doing the above and ensure that everyone you meet at work does the same.
10 Whenever a fraud or near miss occurs, demand that the ERM process is fixed so that it never happens again.

OUR THREE KEY CONCLUSIONS

If fraud risk management works and a workforce is fully Fraud Smart, then there is hope in the fight against employee fraud.

There are three main conclusions that we can draw from our discussions and suggestions in this chapter. These conclusions will be used to drive your Fraud Smart toolkit, which you will be designing at the end of this part of the book:

19.1 Fraud Smart people understand the need to build the theat of fraud into the way in which business objectives are established and implemented within the organization.
19.2 Fraud Smart people integrate fraud risk within the way in which they assess business risk within their area of responsibility.
19.3 Fraud Smart people set high standards of zero tolerance and demand that their managers, their colleagues and their associates do the same.

It is only by being Fraud Smart that everyone who works for or is associated with an organization can appreciate what fraud is and its ramifications. This entails having, at a minimum, the basic knowledge that is contained in this book.

20
Building Your Fraud Smart Toolkit

We have now completed the final part of the Fraud Smart cycle, which is about managing the risk of fraud in a dynamic manner. As you know, this book is based around the Fraud Smart cycle, which covers five key aspects of helping non-specialists get to grips with fraud at work. This is set out in Figure 20.1.

This chapter sits within the fifth part of the Fraud Smart cycle, Mastering Suitable Controls, and covers the task of helping you improve your personal Fraud Smart toolkit.

KEY LEARNING OBJECTIVES

Let's return to the learning objectives that were set for this part of the book:

To describe an integrated fraud risk management process that allows you to assume a Fraud Smart approach to work.

OUR FRAUD CYCLE

Mastering Suitable Controls

Understanding the Threat

Recognizing Red Flags

Appreciating Respective Roles

Embracing Sound Ethics

Figure 20.1   The Fraud Smart cycle.

This chapter gives you the chance to reflect on the key conclusions that have been developed in the chapters in this part of the book and how they can become part of your personal development strategy.

Key Conclusions	Personal Fraud Smart Toolkit
17.1 The board should ensure that fraud control is a key part of the overall control framework and that it fits with the main components, which in our case use the well-known COSO format.	Have a look at your organization's version of its control framework. This should be on the intranet and in published financial statements. Look at www.coso.org for further information on control frameworks. Don't assume that this is nothing to do with you, as internal control is really the collective actions of everyone in the organization.
17.2 Each management team should ensure that it is reviewing fraud risk and associated controls on a regular basis to discharge its role in the anti-fraud policy.	At the next team meeting, raise the topic of fraud and make sure that it is addressed as a possible threat if this relates to any of the topics under discussion. This is particularly the case when procedures, changes to business systems and staffing or new projects are being addressed.

(Continued)

Key Conclusions	Personal Fraud Smart Toolkit
17.3 Efforts to establish fraud control cycles should be monitored for effectiveness and each manager will want to share any appropriate information and advice across all business lines.	Talk to colleagues in other parts of the business and ask them how they deal with fraud control and new threat alerts. If you read about a new fraud threat that could affect your organization, you really must bring this information back to work. Being a Fraud Smart organization means that everyone is on the lookout for external and internal fraud. It is a sad fact that fraudsters will target the weakest organizations and avoid those that are better protected, more alert and Fraud Smart.
18.1 Everyone should appreciate the dynamics of controls that safeguard against fraud with a view to preventing and detecting potential and actual fraud and abuse.	Do some research into internal control. Any search engine will bring up interesting results in terms of authoritative material. Consider in particular controls that guard against the risk of fraud.
18.2 Everyone should be aware of the limitations of controls that mean that they cannot be relied on to prevent all frauds all the time.	Controls cannot protect against all risks and all possible frauds. The extent of the controls in place relates to the risk appetite that drives the business strategy and resulting processes. Do some research into the fascinating topic of 'risk appetites'. One question that is asked is: Is the cost of controls more expensive than the risks against which they seek to guard? This question is a fair business response, but failing to control fraud means that it will grow and writing off the result may look a bit like engaging in conspiracy to defraud.

Key Conclusions	Personal Fraud Smart Toolkit
18.3 Everyone should be able to understand and work with basic controls that guard against fraud and appreciate the way in which these controls work in practice.	List the type of controls that are in place in your work area and assess whether they are being used properly. Talk to your boss about any concerns in this respect. Anti-fraud controls must work or we are all in trouble. If you are aware of any flaws, you need to speak up. In this instance, silence can once again look a bit like conspiracy to defraud, if a fraud were to arise.
19.1 Fraud Smart people understand the need to build the threat of fraud into the way in which business objectives are established and implemented within the organization.	Prepare a short paper setting out how Fraud Smart people are able to relate fraud risk management to the way in which business objectives are set and implemented in your organization. Set this task as part of your performance targets to present this paper to your next team meeting.
19.2 Fraud Smart people integrate fraud risk within the way in which they assess business risk within their area of responsibility.	Prepare a short paper setting out how Fraud Smart people are able to relate fraud risk management to the way in which business risk is addressed in your organization. Set this task as part of your performance targets to present this paper to the next annual staff conference. As well as reading this book, look at the two publications we refer to: *Managing the Business Risk of Fraud: A Practical Guide* and the *Report to the Nations (On Occupational Fraud and Abuse) 2010 Global Fraud Study*.

(Continued)

Key Conclusions	Personal Fraud Smart Toolkit
19.3 Fraud Smart people set high standards of zero tolerance and demand that their managers, their colleagues and their associates do the same.	Being Fraud Smart is not about being suspicious of everyone with whom you work. It does not involve spying on staff and colleagues, nor does it mean that you worry about making friends at work in case one of them may turn out to be deceitful. What it does mean is that you understand the threat of fraud and why some people slip up and go down this path – and what you should do about it if you suspect that it is happening. You understand what might alert you that something is wrong, although strong controls should prevent problems in the first place. But, more than that, you accept that it is part of your duty to live up to the standards in your code of business ethics and to encourage others to do so as well. If you want a real challenge, then ask your boss if you could prepare a short paper setting out how Fraud Smart people are able to promote the fight against fraud in your organization. Set this task as part of your performance targets to file this paper on the corporate intranet under 'Fraud control – a staff member's perspective'. If you do all the tasks in the Fraud Smart personal toolkit in Parts I to V of this book, you will be well on the way to being Fraud Smart. Well done!

You can consider building your Fraud Smart toolkit and decide whether any of the above tasks should be incorporated into your personal development plan that is agreed with your boss.

Fraudsters can be very smart and we all need to be just that bit smarter in the fight against fraud. Now have a go at the final multichoice quiz for Part V of this book, check your answers against Appendix B and record your score in Appendix C.

PART V MULTICHOICE QUIZ

81 Insert the missing word.

. . . . is the most proactive fraud-fighting measure. The design and implementation of control activities should be a coordinated effort spearheaded by management with an assembled cast of employees.

a awareness
b prevention
c detection
d investigation

82 Insert the missing words.

The control environment is what some call the . . . . , which sets the agenda for good control and the standards of conduct that are detailed in the code of ethics.

a top agenda
b big society
c top control
d tone at the top

83 Which is the most appropriate statement?

a Moreover, controls cost money and tend to speed things up. If an agent has to get decisions approved by a more senior person, this means that a deal can become stalled until it is signed off – while the new customer may get frustrated and threaten to walk away from the deal. However, if no approval is required the sales agent could plant a false account into the system.

b Moreover, controls cost money and tend to slow things down. If an agent has to get decisions approved by a more senior person, this means that a deal can become stalled until it is signed off – while the new customer may get frustrated and threaten to walk away from the deal. However, if no approval is required the sales agent could plant a false account into the system.

c Moreover, controls cost money and tend to slow things down. If an agent has to get decisions approved by a more senior person, this means that a deal can become stalled until it is signed off – while the new customer may get frustrated and threaten to walk away from the deal. However, if approval is

required the sales agent could plant a false account into the
system.

d Moreover, controls cost money and tend to slow things down.
If an agent has to get decisions approved by a less senior person,
this means that a deal can become stalled until it is signed off
– while the new customer may get frustrated and threaten to
walk away from the deal. However, if no approval is required
the sales agent could plant a false account into the system.

84 Insert the missing words.
. . . . is about looking at each work area in
question and judging to what extent fraud could occur.
a Risk assessment
b Fraud detection
c The control cycle
d Business analysis

85 Which is the most appropriate statement?
a So the context has been considered in terms of the overall risk
assessment. Fraud risks have been assessed and now specific
controls can be devised or existing ones reviewed to address the
threat of specific frauds.
b So the context has been considered in terms of the overall
control environment. Fraud risks have been managed and now
specific controls can be devised or existing ones reviewed to
address the threat of specific frauds.
c So the context has been considered in terms of the overall
control environment. Fraud risks have been assessed and now
specific controls can be devised or existing ones reviewed to
address the threat of specific frauds.
d So the threat has been considered in terms of the overall control
environment. Fraud risks have been assessed and now specific
controls can be devised or existing ones reviewed to address the
threat of specific frauds.

86 Which is the least appropriate statement?
Controls should:
a Stop innovation in seeking the best business decisions.
b Prevent significant fraud from ever happening.
c Detect any frauds that, despite our best efforts, have still pierced
our defences.

d Respond to these frauds by cleaning up the damage, dealing with the culprit, recovering lost funds and tightening up weak controls that allowed the fraud to happen in the first place.

87 Insert the missing word.
Monitoring is partly about reviewing controls and making sure that the COSO cycle is working well. But it is also about giving . . . . that all is well. So monitoring is not just having a look at the way in which fraud is managed, it can also be a formal process for checking and reporting back that each management team is discharging the corporate policy on fraud control.
a pledges
b assurances
c promises
d guarantees

88 Insert the missing words.
A final weapon is . . . . as a great way of spreading the way in which managers are dealing with this issue across different business lines and support teams.
a expert consultants
b staff gossip
c social events
d fraud awareness training

89 Which is the most appropriate statement?
a Though it is important for organizations to have strategic and effective anti-fraud controls in place, internal controls will prevent all fraud from occurring, and they detect most fraud once it begins.
b Though it is important for organizations to have strategic and effective anti-fraud controls in place, internal controls will not prevent all fraud from occurring, nor will they detect most fraud once it begins.
c Though it is important for organizations to have strategic and effective anti-fraud controls in place, internal controls will prevent all fraud from occurring, but they may not detect most fraud once it begins.
d Though it is important for organizations to have strategic and effective anti-fraud controls in place, internal controls will

never prevent fraud from occurring, nor will they detect any
fraud once it begins.

90 What is being referred to?
    This is the simple act of making sure that everything that happens
    in an organization is supposed to happen; that is, that the activity
    fits the criteria set for what have been agreed as official activities
    approved by management.
    a Authorization
    b Reconciliation
    c Recording
    d Audit trail

91 Insert the missing words.
    . . . . are there to ensure that there is a consistent
    response to transactions, enquiries, orders, projects, new
    developments, recruiting staff, training, performance appraisal,
    planning, marketing products, researching new ventures – the list
    goes on and on.
    a Supervisors
    b Procedures
    c Incentives
    d Counsellors

92 Insert the missing words.
    Supervision is important where staff are dealing with . . . .
    . . . . such as cash, accounting records, contract negotiations,
    overseas permits, software engineering and a whole range of other
    parts of the business.
    a cash-based items
    b staff-related issues
    c portable items
    d high-risk areas

93 What is being referred to?
    The idea is to ensure that no one person has an excessive amount
    of control over transactions, resources or decisions, in order to
    ensure that they cannot embark on fraud without colluding with
    others. It also means that they will not readily be able to conceal
    a fraud.

    a Supervision of work
    b Segregation of duties
    c Examination of output
    d Reconciliation of transactions

94 Insert the missing words.

A structured fraud risk assessment, tailored to the organization's size, complexity, industry and goals, should be performed and updated periodically. The assessment may be integrated with an overall . . . . or performed as a stand-alone exercise, but should, at a minimum, include risk identification, risk likelihood and significance assessment, and risk response.

    a organizational risk assessment
    b staff meetings plan
    c performance appraisal system
    d disciplinary procecure

95 Insert the missing words.

Our model is held together by the concept of . . . .
. . . . , which makes sure that risk-based steps to improve controls and promote success are brought together through a structured rather than haphazard approach to this task.

    a control risk assessment
    b management review
    c enterprise risk management
    d internal auditing

96 Which is the least appropriate statement?

    a The worst way to deal with fraud and abuse is to relate it to business goals.
    b Each organization will have set goals that it needs to achieve and will have to report back to stakeholders on how it is getting on with these achievements.
    c If the goals are based on wide-ranging concepts that adopt a long-term focus, making sure that ethics is at the centre of everything and that the corporate reputation is protected and enhanced, then it is easy to see where fraud risk management fits in.
    d Where objectives are linked only to short-term income targets, there is less incentive to engage in fraud risk assessment.

97 Insert the missing words.
    The . . . . will ask the organization to
    define its view on fraud and how it expresses this view to its
    stakeholders.
    a zero tolerance policy
    b code of ethics
    c anti-fraud policy
    d efficiency review plan

98 Which is the least appropriate item?
    The anti-fraud strategy will include all the usual items, including
    such topics as:
    a Policy aim and ownership, board approval and review process
    b Board's role and involvement and roles and responsibilities
       across the organization
    c Internal audit plan
    d Fraud reporting channels and data mining and other fraud-
       detection tools

99 Insert the missing word.
    Because of the nature of . . . . within fraud, we also
    need an ongoing search for concealed frauds that are happening
    undetected, which means that detection routines are an important
    part of the overall strategy:
    a illegality
    b deceit
    c losses
    d loopholes

100 Insert the missing word, which appears four times.
    This is a crucial stage, as an investigation is about uncovering the
    truth and securing . . . . that is sufficient, reliable and
    convincing enough to support subsequent charges using the
    rigorous standards of the criminal justice system. Tainted . . . . .
    . . . is . . . . that has lost its integrity, infringes the rights of
    the suspect or simply breaches the rules of . . . . gathering
    set by criminal law, which means that it might get thrown out of
    court.
    a facts
    b evidence
    c paperwork
    d surveillance

Appendix A
Corporate Fraud Smart Policy

AIM OF THE FRAUD SMART POLICY

The corporate Fraud Smart policy aims to ensure that the risk of fraud is minimized through the implementation of the Fraud Smart risk cycle. This seeks to equip our workforce with the relevant understanding and tools required to protect the reputation of our organization.

Our goal is to help raise awareness among non-specialists to help get everyone involved in the fight against fraud. We have set a *zero tolerance* for all behaviour that breaches or may appear to breach criminal laws, our code of conduct and/or our policies and procedures at work. We aim to succeed in fighting fraud and not see our reputation suffer by becoming a target. We will do this by making sure that everyone:

- Understands the threat of fraud.
- Appreciates their role in fighting fraud.
- Embraces a sound moral compass.
- Recognizes red flags that suggest that fraud may be happening.
- Is part of the process for ensuring that sound controls are in place to guard against the risk of fraud.

Our employees should have a good understanding of the risk of fraud and its potential impact on the organization, along with how this risk can be managed.

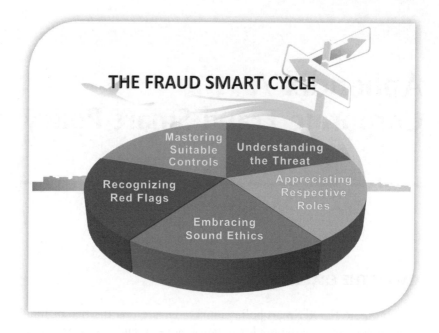

Figure A.1   The Fraud Smart cycle.

DEFINING FRAUD

Fraud is defined as:

Any act or omission involving deceit that attempts to deceive others, in a way that results in the victim suffering a loss and/or the perpetrator achieving a gain.

Other definitions that are relevant are that corruption involves using one's position to obtain any unlawful benefit, while straightforward theft is about depriving the rightful owner of their property. Fraud affects at least four main aspects of our organization: our income received, our spending, our data (or information) and our assets.

- Income is an obvious target for fraudsters, in the sense that if it can be diverted into someone's bank account then it becomes the income of the beneficiary. The key question to ask is: Can funds due to our organization be intercepted and diverted?

- Expenditure is also a target, in that fraudsters will try to achieve payment to themselves (or an associate) by diverting funds so that they fall under their control. The key question to ask is: Can our payments be activated so that they end up in the fraudster's account, or be misapplied in any way?
- The theft of company assets can become widespread if it is not controlled. The key question to ask is: What assets are at risk and can they be accessed in an inappropriate manner?
- Data, personal information and company intelligence present a growing problem in terms of the fraud angle. The key question to ask is: How can we protect the vast amount of information held on our corporate and local systems?

Frauds can be simple scams that happen just by chance or they can be based around an intricate web of deceit, involving, say, the misstatement of financial accounts that on face value may not appear to be illegal. They can be perpetrated by employees or arise from criminals with no relationship to the organization. Within this matrix are many different combinations, including collusion between an employee and an outsider, which mean that the threat is ever changing.

Global markets and online business are designed to promote successful business growth by exploiting foreign markets and e-commerce, which may increase the scope for fraudsters worldwide to exploit our systems. Cyber-terrorism is an adjunct to fraud and we also need to protect our systems against sabotage and blackmail.

Fraud can involve several different types of activities, for example:

- Intentional manipulation of financial statements.
- Misappropriation of tangible assets and misuse of resources.
- Corruption involving bribery and gratuities.

Fraud will definitely happen if four factors coincide:

- *Benefit.* Fraud involves deceit to gain some sort of advantage, which means that there must be some benefit derived from committing the fraud. Whenever something goes wrong, the first course of action is to explore the possibility of simple error. Once this has been ruled out, then it may be an idea to pose the question: Who benefits from this activity? The response may well point to fraud as a possibility.

- *Access*. There are numerous assets and interests that have to be protected by any organization to prevent fraud. The next ingredient of fraud relates to access, since fraud can only happen when the fraudster is able to access the benefit or gain that they are after. Access is about having an opportunity to commit fraud.
- *Motive*. Even if there is some benefit to be gained from taking a deceitful course of action and an employee can access the system or transaction in question, fraud will not necessarily occur. The employee will need to be motivated to commit fraud for fraud to happen. Motive means having a reason to do something along with an intent to do it.
- *Concealment*. The final ingredient relates to concealment, or what we can call the art of not getting caught. The ability to conceal a fraud tends to be related to the way in which controls can be overriden or records falsified to make it seem that there are no discrepancies.

The bottom line is that if the right set of circumstances come together at the right time, illegality will be the most probable result. Fraud can be perpetrated by employees, suppliers, customers, criminal gangs and associates. Nevertheless, it is wrong to assume everyone is dishonest all the time; since the essence of business is based around mutual trust, that would mean that no one would do business with anyone. It is simply the case that deceit can undermine a business relationship, and we need to be aware that given the right set of circumstances, some people may succumb to temptation.

FRAUD SMART ROLES

Fighting fraud involves all our employees. Everyone, including non-specialists, needs to have some knowledge of the Fraud Smart policy, fraud prevention, fraud detection and also how to respond if a fraud is suspected in the workplace. This concept should also apply to partners, agents, consultants, associates, contractors, key suppliers and anyone who has a close working relationship with our organization.

The entire workforce should be aware of the following:

- What is fraud?
- Why does it pose a threat to all organizations?
- What do our values and ethics say?

- What roles do we have in fraud control?
- How do you help prevent fraud at work?
- How do you report suspicious circumstances?
- What is our stance on discipline and prosecution?
- What is available in terms of fraud awareness training?
- Where can you find the anti-fraud strategy?
- Where can you go for further information?

Each employee and associate should be able to answer these and other related questions to be an effective deterrent against fraud and corruption at work.

Fraud Prevention

As well as a good knowledge of the Fraud Smart policy, every employee should appreciate the way good controls can act as a safeguard against the risk of fraud.

- This includes the need to understand and comply with existing controls that protect resources and ensure that no one person has too much control over sensitive parts of the business. Controls that ensure that transactions are properly approved and that audit trails record who did what are also important.
- There is often very little time to spend on verification and checking routines to make sure that all transactions are valid. In this environment, it is necessary to operate sound controls to keep sight of the need to address the threat of fraud. In terms of respective roles, everyone should know the basics of internal control and the need to tighten controls for high-risk transactions and in high-risk environments.

Fraud Detection

Where controls fail, fraud may happen. Even when good controls are in place, a canny person can work out ways of getting around them to access assets that should have been protected.

- You should be alert to the possibility of an opportunist crime and of ongoing scams. This means that managers, supervisors, work teams and front-line agents should be able to spot a fraud that is either obvious or raises inconsistencies that need to be probed.

- Detection tends to happen when two and two add up to three and questions are asked. When they come to light, many frauds are greeted with a view that staff knew something was wrong but did not think to ask questions. In fact, some frauds start with an employee making a mistake and realizing that no one picks it up. As they go on to repeat this action and remain undetected, they push forwards and commit major acts of misappropriation, knowing that they will not be found out.
- Alert staff who follow up on odd mistakes or unusual incidents can act as a major control in stopping frauds at an early stage or even ensuring that they are not completed at all. Complaints can be a major source of identifying irregularity. A complaint may be made by someone that results from basic error or some form of misunderstanding that has led to a problem. However, after having looked into all these possible causes, a Fraud Smart employee may need to consider the possibility of internal fraud that has led to the discrepancy or anomaly.

Fraud Smart employees understand red flags and various indicators that suggest that fraud may be happening, such as the following:

- *Lifestyle.* If someone is living above their means, there could be a number of quite reasonable explanations, although having lots of money could suggest that an illegal source of funds has been exploited.
- *Position.* More senior people can do much more damage and for longer periods because of their position at work. A tried-and-trusted senior manager will tend to have a great deal of authority to approve transactions, override controls and alter records simply because of their special position, which means that they have access to company resources that most others do not have.
- *Behaviour.* When someone behaves in an unusual manner, this could be the result of many different factors, for example that they are simply awkward and that is that. Or it could be that their behaviour is designed to distract or even stop anyone from examining their activities and finding out that something is wrong. How a business activity is conducted can also be an indication of fraud and red flags can include missing files, altered records, odd journal transfers, photocopies in files, unusual patterns of transactions and a whole assortment of oddities.

Fraud Response

The final aspect of the workforce's role in fraud control relates to responding to frauds that have been detected:

- It is important that we all know how to respond to an actual or suspected fraud. In most cases, the response will be to inform an immediate line manager or, failing that, an authorized person, which in our case is internal audit. For more senior employees, some knowledge of the way in which frauds are investigated may also be required, as the investigators may require cooperation and assistance as they search for and review the available evidence. The appendix at the end of this policy goes over our approach to Fraud Smart investigations. In no circumstances should you undertake your own investigation into a suspicious activity.
- If you suspect a fraud, do not check what is on the suspect's computer. If someone boots up the computer of a suspected fraudster, they become the last person to activate the computer, which may undermine a future prosecution that depends on what files the defendant had accessed on their work computer.
- Do not go through a suspect's personal possessions in a company locker or desk. If the suspect's personal possessions are searched, it may infringe crucial privacy rules and again may undermine management's response to the allegations and taint anything found in the search.
- Do not discuss a suspect's guilt. If a case is discussed with a friend, it may become defamation in seeking to damage the reputation of the suspect based on unsubstantiated allegations or suspicions.
- One final consideration is the way in which control weaknesses will need to be closed when a fraud is discovered and this will be part of the fraud response strategy. There may be a need for a quick fix, in terms of freezing certain accounts or changing access facilities to certain systems; then there will be a planned response, to tighten up controls as part of a longer-term solution.

As a Fraud Smart employee you should should report all suspicions and be prepared to get involved in correcting any poor controls in areas for which you are responsible.

Specialist Roles

There are several specialist roles in respect of managing the risk of fraud:

- The chief executive officer has overall responsibility for ensuring that the risk of fraud is properly addressed in our organization.
- The director of XYZ owns the Fraud Smart policy and is responsible for ensuring that it is implememented across the organization, which includes the anti-fraud strategy, fraud response plan and staff training programmes.
- The audit committee is responsible for providing oversight of the extent to which the Fraud Smart policy is achieving its set aims.
- Each line manager is responsible for ensuring that the Fraud Smart policy is being observed in their work area and that the risk of fraud is properly understood and effectively managed.
- The chief internal auditor does not have primary responsibility for managing the risk of fraud, but must ensure that this risk is fully addressed during audit work and may review how far managers are adhering to the Fraud Smart policy. Moreover, the CIA is responsible for conducting periodic tests (such as data mining) that seek to detect complicated fraud and will investigate all allegations of fraud on behalf of the director of XYZ.
- Likewise, the external auditor does not have primary responsibility for managing the risk of fraud, but must ensure that this risk is fully addressed during audit work and will be alert to red flags that suggest a fraud may be occurring. The external auditor will be on guard for material frauds that affect the reliability of the financial accounts.
- The head of human resources and legal officer will be involved in decisions about how allegations of fraud against employees are investigated and how sanctions are applied.
- The press office will be the point of contact for anyone enquiring about a fraud that affects our organization.

FRAUD SMART COMPETENCIES

Solid fraud control involving all levels of employees will only work when the skills needed to underpin the Fraud Smart concept have been established, which involves everyone achieving the level of competence described below.

Compliant

Procedures and routines seek to ensure the smooth conduct of our business so that risk is minimized and corporate resources are protected. A culture of complying with set controls is extremely important and each member of staff must act in accordance with our procedures. All employees must report actual or suspected breaches of procedure. Remember that being Fraud Smart is not about being suspicious of everyone and everything, it just means being proactive in protecting our resources.

Honest

Each employee needs to ensure that they can live up to the expectations that are set out in the corporate Code of Ethics. We believe that setting high standards is about having a good 'tone at the top', right from board level, and then driving this concept down into the organization through example and encouragement. All employees should adhere to the Code of Ethics, which includes the following:

- *Integrity*. Employees and associates are expected to behave in an honest and fair way at all times.
- *Accountability*. The entire workforce is expected to stand up and be counted for its actions in seeking to safeguard the integrity of our resources.
- *Transparency*. All business decisions should be made in an acceptable manner with no conflict of interest, so that any resultant risks and exposures can be clearly appreciated by our stakeholders.

The Code of Ethics should inspire our workforce to make the 'right' decisions that keep the business within our accepted risk appetite. As such, all suitable measures should be employed to make sure that everyone knows about the code, that it is fully understood and that everyone is able to live up to its requirements. Appropriate sanctions, including dismissal, will be considered where an employee has breached the Code of Ethics. When an employee fraud has occurred, the disciplinary code must swing into action; even if a criminal conviction is not achieved at court (or even attempted), the employee in question may still be dismissed if they are shown to have breached our Code of Ethics.

Competent

The board of directors should possess the skills required to cope with the demands of a fast-changing business and live up to their duty to protect the corporate resource, while all managers and staff should be appropriately trained to understand how controls guard against fraud and how these controls can be breached. Competent employees are well placed to stand their ground when there is a chance that their work and decisions might be examined during any internal or external fraud investigation.

Astute

Every employee should have a really good understanding of the nature of fraud, the risk it poses and the way in which the organization faces this risk through the Fraud Smart policy and resulting strategy. Astute people look out for red flags and know that custody of money, assets, funds and personal data should be verified through suitable security measures. Moreover, astute people know the dangers of talking in public about confidential business matters.

Staff Training

Every employee should possess the requisite level of knowledge and skills to implement the corporate Fraud Smart policy. There should be in place a variety of assessment measures agreed with your line management to determine your training needs. Assessments can involve whatever sources are agreed, such as personal judgement, colleagues' feedback (or feedback from peer groups), performance targets, comments from customers and so on. The final stage is to list the actions needed to close any gap that has been defined through this analysis. The book *Fraud Smart* (John Wiley & Sons) represents a minimum level of knowledge for each member of staff. A simple table can be used to assist in this process:

Table A.1 Anti-fraud attributes self-analysis.

Anti-fraud personal attribute	Desired level of knowledge and skills	Actual level of knowledge and skills	Personal development action required
COMPLIANT	1 Aware of all relevant policies and procedures. 2 Able to apply relevant operational procedures. 3 Understands compliance routines applied across the business lines.		
HONEST	1 Aware of all aspects of business ethics. 2 Able to reconcile tensions within ambiguous situations. 3 Provides leadership in ethical behaviour. 4 Able to challenge decisions that expose a conflict of interests.		
COMPETENT	1 Possesses the required knowledge, qualifications and experience for the job. 2 Undertakes fraud awareness training wherever appropriate. 3 Seeks to improve anti-fraud controls.		
ASTUTE	1 Understands the nature of deceit and how it may manifest itself. 2 Able to negotiate around trusting people while also holding a healthy professional scepticism. 3 Alert to red flags that indicate fraud may be happening and prepared to report any reasonable suspicions.		
OTHER	1 Understands the contents and guidance in the *Fraud Smart* book.		

FRAUD SMART REPORTING

We ask all our employees to report concerns at work involving allegations of fraud and corruption, although any abuse of this facility for personal reasons may become a disciplinary offence. Every manager should ensure that their staff know the reporting procedure and understand how they can make use of hotlines and that they have a duty to report all suspicions. If you have any concerns at work, please talk to your line manager as the first point of contact unless:

- The matter is too complex, involving many different parts of the business.
- The manager is away or there is a vacancy at that level.
- The manager may be implicated.
- The matter has already been referred to the manager with no real resolution.
- You have been asked to provide information to an authorized person in the whistleblowing procedure.

It is hoped that most concerns will find their way to the line manager and be resolved immediately through the normal management channels. Most importantly, each manager should operate an 'open-door policy' wherever feasible to encourage team members to come forward and discuss any concerns at work.

The Fraud Smart employee has to tread carefully. Being Fraud Smart means recognizing that some people, some of the time, will be tempted to engage in illegality. However, that does not mean that the manager's office becomes the scene of a series of clandestine meetings where team members take turns to accuse each other of being unfair or being a little odd or suspicious. There are occasions when the whistleblowing hotline may be the best way of ensuring that wrongdoing is addressed and, as such, we have installed the following facility:

- Dedicated reporting line manned by professionals.
- Convenient manned 24-hour service.
- The informer will be given ongoing feedback about progress.
- The director of XYZ will monitor how the whistleblowing line is being used.

You may view information on the fraud reporting line at xxx. If you have experienced problems using this facility, please contact the director of XYZ on . . . .

FRAUD SMART CONTROLS

The Fraud Smart approach is based on good controls that are designed and applied to fight fraud and seek to:

- Prevent significant fraud from ever happening.
- Detect any frauds that, despite our best efforts, have still pierced our defences.
- Respond to these frauds by cleaning up the damage, dealing with the culprit, recovering lost funds and tightening up weak controls that allowed the fraud to happen in the first place.

Basic Controls

There are several well-known mechanisms for combating the threat of fraud. As that threat alters, the way in which these mechanisms are employed should be adjusted accordingly.

- *Authorization* is the simple act of making sure that everything that happens in an organization is supposed to happen; that is, the activity fits the criteria set for what have been agreed as official activities approved by management. The key question to ask is: How can we ensure that unauthorized transactions do not make it through our systems?
- *Exception reporting and audit trails* are both preventive controls, in that they deter employees from attempting suspect transactions, and detective controls that will hopefully pick up suspect items that have got through. The key question to ask is: How can we best pick up suspect or incorrect activities through our system tools and checking routines?
- *Procedures* cover just about everything that happens in an organization that needs to happen in a set manner to ensure that there is a consistent response to, for example, transactions, enquiries, placing orders, projects, new developments, recruiting staff, training, performance appraisal, planning, marketing products, researching new ventures – the list goes on and on. Our corporate procedures are also extremely important, such as the scheme of delegation, investment appraisal, budgetary controls, accounting rules, financial regulations, gifts register and the procurement code. The key question to ask is: Do our procedures work in ensuring that the risk of fraud is minimized?

- *Verification* is a key control over fraud and abuse. This is about checking that a representation is what it purports to be. The key question to ask is: Is this person who they say they are and how can we be sure?
- *Supervision* is also important. Managers have to keep an eye on their staff and supervisors need to monitor their team members. The question to ask is: Are our high-risk areas adequately supervised?
- *Segregation of duties* is a basic control concept that means that no one person has an excessive amount of control over transactions, resources or decisions, in order to ensure that they cannot embark on fraud without colluding with others. It also means that the person in question will readily not be able to conceal a fraud. The key question for this control is: How can we ensure that our employees do not have an excessive degree of influence over high-risk areas of the business that would make the prospect of fraud more likely to arise and be concealed?

Fraud Smart Risk Management

Fraud Smart risk management starts with our objectives and business strategy. This approach is aimed at countering the basic problem with anti-fraud measures, where some employees feel that these measures are not related to their role in seeking to achieve business goals. They are seen as 'nice-to-have' rather than 'must-have' measures. The best way to deal with fraud and abuse is to relate it to business goals. Anti-fraud risk efforts should therefore flow from the business strategy by arguing that success can only happen within a culture that promotes honesty while also tackling any dishonesty within our workforce.

Effective fraud risk management has a pivotal focus on threat assessment. The logic is simple. If we are able to identify all the different types of fraud and security breaches we could suffer, we can then make sure that each threat is countered through a set of solid corporate defence mechanisms. Threat assessment must be built into the way people carry out their business as a natural way of working and getting the job done. In this scenario, threat assessment should be part of the ongoing process of looking at risks and emerging issues in which every manager and work team should be involved, before they are able to update their business risk management strategy and risk registers.

The idea is to work with your colleagues and team members to ensure that there is a robust risk register in place that also addresses fraud risks and sets out how controls may be improved to guard against risks to the achievement of business objectives. Because of the nature of deceit, we also need an ongoing search for concealed frauds that are happening undetected, which means that detection routines should be an important part of the overall strategy.

Please note that whenever the risk log is updated by the line manager and/or business support teams, the threat of existing and emerging frauds should be incorporated within the risk assessments and ensuing risk management strategies.

Fraud Smart risk management is an all-consuming process that sucks in risks from all parts of the organization and seeks to have these risks assessed and managed in a structured manner. The equation is quite straightforward and can be summed up in 10 simple tasks:

1 Have in place an integrated method for managing risk that is driven by our adopted business strategy and is there to drive success through the organization.
2 Take ownership of fraud risk management by being Fraud Smart.
3 Adopt zero tolerance of fraud based on the adopted code of business ethics and state that it will not be allowed to happen here or there will be stiff consequences.
4 Make sure that the threat of fraud is assessed in a rigorous and dynamic manner.
5 Build the threat of fraud into the way business risk is assessed and managed through our business risk management process.
6 Improve controls, tighten loopholes and do not base controls on the assumption that everyone is trustworthy at all times. Review the use of basic controls such as authorization that were outlined earlier.
7 Check that your people are complying with these controls.
8 Talk to your staff about fraud risk management and train them to be Fraud Smart.
9 Keep doing the above and ensure that everyone you meet at work does the same.
10 Whenever a fraud or near miss occurs in your work area, you should ensure that your risk management arrangements are reviewed so that it never happens again.

APPENDIX: FRAUD SMART INVESTIGATIONS

We need to ensure that there is an effective response to frauds that have arisen. Below is an outline of our approach to investigating fraud:

- *Preliminary assessment.* As soon as a fraud comes to light, it is essential that the fraud response plan swings into action. This may involve the legal team, human resources, the director for the area in question and the investigating team, which in our case is internal audit. The question to address is: Has a fraud actually happened?
- *Initial response and threat control.* The first response will involve making sure that the right people are informed, securing the evidence, ensuring confidentiality, looking for additional fraud threats as the picture emerges and quickly fixing any controls that have failed.
- *Interim report.* A formal report should be drawn up dealing with the matters mentioned above for consideration by the key decision maker, which, wherever feasible, will be the relevant director (for the area affected by the fraud) with advice from legal and human resources. The board and audit committee will also be informed. It may be possible to freeze bank accounts for the suspect(s) in question.
- *Investigation plan and police role.* An investigation team and lead investigator should be appointed. The police may be asked for a view on the case and whether they will be involved at this early stage of events.
- *Full investigation.* The main investigation will be carried out with a view to securing the available evidence and discovering the truth. The employee in question may be suspended if the evidence would otherwise be at risk or, on occasion, the investigation may start out as covert in order to secure live evidence if this is seen as the best way forward.
- *Securing evidence.* This is a crucial stage of the investigation and is about uncovering the truth and securing evidence that is sufficient, reliable and convincing enough to support subsequent charges using the rigorous standards of the criminal justice system. Tainted evidence is evidence that has lost its integrity, infringes the rights of the suspect or simply breaches the rules of evidence gathering set by criminal law, which means that it might get thrown out of court.
- *Interviewing.* Witnesses, colleagues, managers and others will be interviewed to secure evidence that supports the investigation by shedding light on the allegations.

- *Confidentiality and media contact.* During the course of the investigation regard will be paid to confidentiality and how the media will be informed about events. It is best to use one channel of communication, which in our case is the press office, in order to control the proceedings and guard against defamation and excessive damage to the corporate reputation.
- *Action options.* The investigation will result in a report that will give direction about possible criminal proceedings, with referral to the local police and/or staff disciplinary procedures for gross misconduct. The disciplinary action may be based around breach of procedure and possible dismissal at an early stage if there is sufficient evidence regarding the conduct of the employee. Meanwhile, the police case will focus on criminal charges and a possible conviction, which may take time to conclude.
- *Recovery.* Throughout the investigation the question of recovery and damage limitation will be assessed, although offers for the return of funds by the suspect will have to be discussed with the company lawyers.
- *Control fixes.* While the above investigation is progressing, management should be involved in fixing weaknesses in internal controls as part of the ongoing risk management process.

Fraud Smart people should not be intimately involved in this type of work, which should be done by people specially trained in forensic examination. However, anyone may be called on to cooperate with an ongoing fraud investigation.

Appendix B
Multichoice Quiz: Answers

Check your answers against the answer guide below.

1 b	26 b	51 b	76 a
2 a	27 a	52 d	77 c
3 c	28 b	53 b	78 b
4 d	29 d	54 d	79 d
5 a	30 b	55 a	80 b
6 c	31 b	56 c	81 b
7 d	32 d	57 b	82 d
8 b	33 c	58 b	83 b
9 d	34 c	59 d	84 a
10 c	35 a	60 b	85 c
11 c	36 d	61 c	86 a
12 a	37 b	62 b	87 b
13 d	38 b	63 a	88 d
14 b	39 b	64 d	89 b
15 a	40 a	65 d	90 a
16 c	41 b	66 b	91 b
17 b	42 c	67 a	92 d
18 c	43 a	68 c	93 b
19 a	44 d	69 d	94 a
20 c	45 b	70 d	95 c
21 b	46 c	71 b	96 a
22 d	47 a	72 a	97 c
23 a	48 c	73 c	98 c
24 d	49 d	74 d	99 b
25 c	50 a	75 b	100 b

Appendix C
Fraud Smart:
Your Score Sheet

NAME

. . . .

DEPARTMENT

. . . .

	Scores achieved	Date completed
Part I: **Understanding the Threat**		_____
Part II: **Appreciating Respective Roles**		_____
Part III: **Embracing Sound Ethics**		_____

(Continued)

	Scores achieved	Date completed
Part IV: **Recognizing Red Flags**		_____
Part V: **Mastering Suitable Controls**		_____
Total Score		

%

Index